Thank you Val for putting up with my hours of absence whilst I tortured the computer.

Thank you to Cliff Cork, Rosie Luton and my family for their help.

I have endeavoured to attribute owners to their pictures, if I have not done so, it meant I was unable to find them and I apologise for any I missed.

/10

Sean

regards

Barry

'Jamie's Dad'

1

10/21

Publisher: Compass Publishing UK.

Printed by New Perspective, Digital Print, Whitstable.

First published September 2021

ISBN 9 781913 713690

A copy of this book is held at the British Library.

STORIES

A Guest of Nippon............................99

Blown up twice..................................115

Chindit...122

DEMs Gunner…...............................25

Escape from Boulogne.....................35

First battle of Narvik.........................6

HMS Medway....................................53

Loss of HMS Delight.........................58

Luck or Fate......................................63

Never forgotten, HMS Bullen............45

Sinking of HMS Hardy (II)................79

Stalag XXB, POW.............................88

FORWARD

These are twelve emotive stories of survival from the World Wars.

Although some research was done into the background of these stories some are written in the men's own words, some contemporaneously. Some of the stories are raw and shocking and show the trauma that some of these men suffered, but usually hid from friends and loved ones. There was no counselling.

I was chairman of the HMS Cavalier Association at the turn of the century when some of these stories were passed to me by these men. Some expressed the hope that their stories would be safe with me and would not be lost when they were gone. Most if not all, have already passed, and this is one of the reasons this book has been written.

Many of them having seen their friends killed used the expressions for their survival as variously.... "Was it Luck, was it Fate or was it just Written that I should survive when others didn't". You can sometimes help your luck. But when fate intervenes or it is 'written in the stars' you have no control over your destiny. Some still had a sense of guilt that they had survived, and their friends had not.

Some 14,000 men died in destroyers during WWII. In 2007 HRH The Duke of Edinburgh dedicated the last of Britain's WWII destroyers, HMS Cavalier, now preserved at Chatham Historic Dockyard, as a memorial to them.

Steel ships do not last forever, so a bronze memorial plaque was also installed on the dockside which he unveiled.

The large bronze memorial, designed by Kenneth Potts of Malvern, was unveiled and dedicated by HRH The Duke of Edinburgh who had served on similar ships during WWII. On the reverse of the memorial are the names of the 145 destroyers lost in WWII. (author)

HMS Cavalier preserved in Chatham Historic Dockyard, 2021.

FIRST BATTLE OF NARVIK

Leslie J. Smale

10th April 1940

Les was a young seaman on HMS Hardy in 1940 when the ship was involved in what became known as the First Battle of Narvik in Norway. He wrote of his experience immediately after his return to England. What follows is written contemporaneously in his own words.

"I will while the events are still alive in my memory attempt to give a description of events, which brought me to take part in the battle of Narvik. My ship, HMS Hardy, H87, left Scapa Flow on the evening of 2nd April 1940 together with the remainder of her division bound for the Shetlands. A little after we had left the boom defences, the air raid defences of Scapa opened up on the dozen or so raiders who were darting around in the almost dark. A heavier barrage I had never seen, the sky literally looked like it had black measles. This was our first raid and naturally we were all anxious to have a crack at them, but with all our beckoning we couldn't persuade them to come near enough to open fire. On the whole, I guess we were quite a bit disappointed, still though we did not know it, our chance was to come…. and soon.

HMS Hardy

Though cold it was quite calm when we arrived at Sullam Voe *(Shetlands)*. The next morning, and after oiling with the destroyer HMS Hunter alongside us, we went to anchor. It was now the 3rd April and no one seemed to know exactly why we were there or for that matter where we were going. However captain D was not slow to take advantage of the lovely weather and took the time to exercise general drills to the utmost. Action stations, landing parties, boarding parties were also items in the programme.

Boarding parties were exercised even to the extent of HMS Hotspur flying a Swastika.

During Friday evening of the 5th four of the 'T' class

destroyers arrived well loaded with mines, following which came all kinds of rumour as to where we were to escort these minelayers. Well, next morning at 0400hrs we weighed anchor and put to sea and at about 0800 we rendezvoused with the battle cruiser HMS Renown. Soon we all settled down in our allotted positions and to a course of something east of north. The sea was very heavy and so was the rain, and by the next morning one couldn't but help feel the nip in the air. This being a Sunday we had our usual little church service on the mess deck, after which lower deck was cleared and Captain Warburton-Lee disclosed that during the afternoon we were crossing the Arctic circle, to which he dryly commented that this called for the same procedure as the 'crossing of the line'. Our final destination he said was a little south of Narvik (*Norway*), where we were to lay mines at dawn on Monday morning off Hovenden, 67' 24"N 14' 36"W. All through that day the sea was quite high and it was not until during the night that it began to ease down and only then because we were getting near land. Dawn on Monday the 8th broke with us at action stations and violating Norwegian neutrality. (*Operation Wilfred force VW*). The mines were all laid within half an hour of the planned time, so despite the weather we had done our first real job well. All that remained for us to do now was to patrol the mine field and guide Norwegian fishermen around it and capture any German ships trying to pass down through neutral waters, which they had previously been doing. The weather here in the fiord was beautiful, hardly a ripple on the water and everything surrounding us covered in a white blanket of snow. Here we stopped until just after noon, when there came a message from the 'Gloworm' (*destroyer*) that she was being attacked by two enemy ships and was returning their fire. Then all went quiet and nothing more was heard from her. (*It was later learned that the tiny destroyer Glowworm had heroically rammed the German Battleship Hipper and had been sunk. Author*)

Meanwhile, word came for us to join 'Renown' and off we went at full speed. The German fleet was at sea and Blenheims, Hudsons and all sorts of our bombers were out looking for them in an effort to bomb them. Things were warming up and everyone, though they knew what the consequences may be, was rather glad. Things were moving rapidly and it was not many hours before we learned that 'Renown' who, in the meantime, had joined up with our mine laying friends of this morning. The sea was now extremely rough and so, for the night, we took up a formation of line ahead 'Renown' leading with 'Hardy'. 'Hunter', 'Havock', Hotspur' and the mine layers following.

At Dawn the next day as was usual, we went to action stations. There were snowstorms about and it was still very cold. We must be further north than ever. We were going through the usual procedure, when suddenly without any signal the 'Renown' altered course to port. Quite naturally all our bridge staff turned their binoculars in that direction. They need not have done so, for a snowstorm suddenly fell on us and blacked or rather whited everything out. The 'Renown' then relieved our anxiety by signalling with a big light 'Two enemy'. I suppose no one could express their feelings at that moment. Mine were I think a mixture of excitement and expectancy, wondering if it really was enemy and what it would be like to be under fire. We were soon to know for in a moment or two the 'Renown' opened fire with a broadside of 15 inch at the leading ship of the two. The snow had cleared and we could now see them away on the horizon. We, the 'Hardy' and 'Hunter', opened fire at extreme range on the second ship. There was an honest to good fight for perhaps quarter of an hour and during that time we realised that the leading ship of the enemy was a cruiser of the Hipper class, the 'Geneisenau', and the other, engaged by just two tiny destroyers was none other than the huge 'Sharnhorst'. There were splashes all round us but mostly everyone was too busy on his own job to let that worry him. They got a straddle on us and while I was thinking that the next should see us off, it never came. It appeared that they were concentrating on the 'Renown'. There were several good straddles on her and we seemed to be left out of it. Then they turned not towards but away from us, the speed in such big seas as we pursued them was too much for the destroyers to maintain. Several times it seemed that we would break our back so we had to ease down to twelve knots. 'Renown' was still chasing them and as we went along we passed all kinds of wreckage, which was obviously German, a rubber raft and pole attached to a marines cap. By now the enemy was out of sight and as 'Renown' went over the horizon she signalled us to return to our patrol on the mines. By this time we hear that the Germans had invaded Norway and at last we knew their fleet was at sea. On our way back we learned that we had suffered no casualties or damage except that there was seven to eight inches of water on the fore mess deck and everything movable had moved and practically all of it had broken, that is, things that were breakable.

During the lull on the way back we replenished the ready use ammunition lockers and squared off the ship generally. The captain and gunnery officer were full of praise for the way the men behaved and the ship was full of talk of what, probably was, the most exciting moments of most of our lives. It was certainly my most exciting moment up till then.

Instead of returning to our patrol as ordered by 'Renown' we went, due I suppose to signals from Admiralty further north towards Narvik and the Lofoten islands on our port and Norway to starboard. Then came more coded massages from Admiralty and in consequence I was among those detailed from each ship for landing party. We all got rigged out and many set about writing farewell letters in case they did not return. Not knowing how long we may be ashore we all fairly well packed ourselves in with chocolate and cigarettes. The plan was apparently to bombard the harbour and shore batteries of Narvik and then land and take the place over. This idea was squashed however when, a couple of hours later we called at a pilots station some forty miles south of Narvik. Here we learned that we were up against a superior force and to put it in the words of the pilot 'I wouldn't go in there with a force three times as big as yours'. Plans were changed and D2 (Cpt Warburton-Lee) decided on a dawn attack. Plans were drawn up and a method of attack signalled to all the ships concerned That evening when we closed up for a final check over of instruments the alarm bells rang and away we went after what looked like a destroyer. As we neared, it turned away, but we soon overhauled it to find that it was a small fishing boat. That night.... it was now the 9th of April, we continued a patrol of the fiord and at about midnight with everyone at action stations the five ships (The 'Hostile' had joined us during the evening) began to move up toward Narvik. My particular action station was as a member of the gunnery directors crew with a duty to operate the cross level unit. This unit using the distant horizon as datum, measured the angle of ship movement at right angles to the line of fire and fed in an appropriate line correction. Since the close proximity of the fiord shoreline on either side made the unit inoperable I was ordered out of the director to become a bridge messenger and as such was in a ringside seat as it were to see all the action that was to come.

The orders were to sink all ship targets and needless to say everyone was on their toes the whole of the time. It began to snow pretty heavily and we could see neither shore, this made navigation much more difficult. The ASDIC submarine detection gear was used to get echoes from either side of the fiord so that we were able to continue our progress up to Narvik. It was bitterly cold and where we were moving around in a vain effort to keep warm we were forming circles in the ice on the deck. Twice rum and tea rations were brought around and did we need it! Generally a quiet atmosphere surrounded the ship, as was only to be expected in such a tense situation. Once in particular when the gunnery officer (Lt Clark) passed around that we were about to pass a shore battery, everything was particularly quiet, with no one saying a word and only the wash of the ship to stir the apparent peace..

Just about 0400, it was now the morning of the 10th April, in the vicinity of the harbour we made for what we thought was the entrance and stopped just in time when we realized that it wasn't. After a little scout around we eventually found it and as the plan had been to fire on the enemy from the entrance we were all very surprised when the 'Hardy' began to lead the division into the harbour itself. It seemed to be so cheeky and yet here we were doing it. There was already one ship run ashore on our starboard side as we went in, but there were plenty more good ones about for us to sink. Still, merchant ships were small fry at the moment... we were looking for destroyers and a submarine. All our guns had been unfrozen with hot oil on the way up and were loaded ready for anything. Everything seemed to be still very quiet and peaceful but that was all changed a few minutes later when we suddenly sighted a destroyers bows showing from behind a large whaling factory ship. Torpedoes were fired and I guess at least a couple of them found their mark for there was a terrific explosion, together with a vivid semi circular white flash of stars twinkling around the edge. If one could forget what that explosion contained it could be described as being extremely beautiful, but when one thinks of sleeping men being killed outright... then it's different... perhaps though that's not the case with a German. Simultaneously with the explosion we gathered speed and opened fire with the guns. Turning to go out of the harbour, two more destroyers were sighted to starboard and engaged, but being probably still asleep, they didn't at this moment return our fire.

By now 'Hardy' was out of the harbour with the

remainder of the division following around in their turn. A second attack was planned and when, some ten minutes later we re-entered the harbour they were waiting for us, or should I say, some of them were, for some were firing H.A. (*High angle*) and others L.A. (*Low angle)* the Germans didn't know if they were under surface or air attack. It was a crazy sight which greeted us this time around, with stems, sterns, funnels and masts sticking up all over the harbour, marking the graveyard of the ships sunk in the first attack. But for the grimness of the situation it was almost an amusing sight. There was more gunfire from what appeared to be shore batteries, and they were firing ammunition which included tracer, so that you could see it coming towards you...sometimes it exploded in flight while at others it went off on contact with the water. Glancing over the ships side I noticed that there were explosions erupting from the water at various places around the ship, which threw up black clouds of smoke. I thought they might be controlled mines, but I don't know for sure. We came out of the harbour again without any casualties, but with a well-earned scar... a two inch hole in the foremost funnel.

We were all quite happy and very pleased with our work but when the captain ordered yet another attack we weren't quite so keen... it was getting very hot in the harbour and they were more than ready for us this time, for we were greeted well and truly with very heavy gunfire and what seemed to be dozens of tin fish (*torpedoes*). After seeing the effect of our own torpedoes, I know there was no one anxious to see the effect of one of theirs on us. Each time one came for us, full speed ahead was ordered and we turned toward it to present as small a target as possible. On one occasion we had just evaded one only to run into the path of another and I honestly believe that my heart stopped beating as I held my breath, together with everyone else, as we waited helplessly for the explosion to occur. But it never came despite the fact that it passed right under us, and the general belief that German torpedoes were all fitted with magnetic heads. If they did then we owe our lives to our D. G. (*Degaussing Gear*), a device that neutralises the magnetic field inherent in a ship. With that thrill over and two of our foes burning and the shore batteries silenced, we turned from the harbour for the last time. The wreckage in the harbour had to be seen to be believed so I can make no attempt to describe it adequately, other than to say that it was immense.

As we passed the harbour entrance with our guns facing aft and firing a few farewell shots we all felt a certain amount of relief. But then all of a sudden, 'Alarm bearing red 5 degrees' was ordered we were all taken by surprise. There was no need to look for we knew in a moment that we had met the enemy once more and to his advantage. He must have been waiting for us, for in an instant shells were crashing into us. I found myself at the bottom of the ladder behind the wheelhouse and was thrown flat on the deck by a shell, which blew off the steel door on the port side; fragments of the door or shell injured two signalmen who were there with me. I put them into the navigator's cabin on the starboard side by myself. Another salvo crashed in and something hit my head, but I wasn't hurt. Self-preservation I guess took me to the port side but just as I got there the telegraphs man came out of the wheelhouse shouting that the coxswain was dead. I for no reason I can explain went into the wheelhouse and took over the wheel from Lt. Stanning, the paymaster, who said he was going back to the bridge. The wheelhouse was a shambles. It was not till I was actually on the job that I realised the danger I was in, but I consoled myself thinking that if this was my day then it was my day. I felt better. I couldn't make contact with the bridge and my repeated calls through the voice pipe of 'Wheelhouse, Bridge' were unanswered. I was left to my own initiative as to what I should do. Looking through the gaping shell holes in the wheelhouse side I could see for the first time the German ships.

The destruction in the harbour had to be seen to be believed. (U-Boat.net)

There were five of them, two now ahead and three to starboard. We were close to the shore so I steered a course that kept us as close as I dared and hoped we wouldn't go aground. In a little while contact was made to Lt Stanning on the bridge and he ordered 'Hard a starboard, we are going to ram'. I felt fit for anything now, but almost immediately the order was cancelled by 'Hard a port, we are going ashore'. I put the helm over to port. Just as we were about to ground the Midshipman came into the wheelhouse shouting 'You're going aground' and rang the engine room telegraphs to full astern. It had no effect as the engines had lost steam due to a hit in the boilers, and it was because of this loss of power that Lt. Stanning had changed from ramming the enemy ships to taking 'Hardy' ashore. I didn't feel her ground and I think I stood there at the wheel in a dazed condition for two or three minutes until someone came by shouting 'Abandon ship'. I walked, They were not firing at us now, out on to the .5 machine gun deck and helped the two aforementioned injured signalmen into the sea boat. The whaler was full to over flowing with no one on the falls to lower it. Someone did come along to perform this duty and took a turn for lowering, as for a normal boats crew of seven, whereupon the boat went down with a terrific rush and capsized. A Carley float was in the water by now full of survivors and I can remember shouts of 'Anyone got a knife?'… None was forthcoming; It was needed to cut the paddles free. Some men were beginning to reach the beach and I noticed that the swimming distance was not all that far and that one could wade half the journey. Being a fair swimmer I decided I could stay and help where I could so I took off my Duffel coat and oilskin and went to the bridge to give a hand as necessary. The bridge was in a terrible state with the following casualties; Captain seriously wounded in the head and arm and unconscious, Signal officer – dead, Gunnery Officer – dead, Navigator suffering from concussion and the Paymaster with a foot injury. I with the Middy released the telegraphist from his remote control post, the door of which was jammed shut. We then assisted the doctor to bandage the captain and then put him in a Neil Robinson stretcher (a cane wrap around affair to prevent the patient falling out) and lowered him to the forecastle deck.

Wreck of HMS Hardy, she later rolled onto her starboard side. (U-Boat.net)

We then got the navigator clear of the bridge and destroyed what books we though might be of use to the enemy before finally leaving the bridge ourselves. Meanwhile, No 4 gun had been getting up more ammunition and was again firing at the enemy. As I reached the forecastle deck and had just taken up my coat to retrieve any valuables from the pockets, the Germans opened fire on us again and registered a direct hit on No 2 gun, which was already out of action. I dropped flat and felt splinters of metal hitting my tin hat, which undoubtedly saved me from injury. The doctor was injured in this, and the chief stoker was mortally wounded. Having retrieved my valuables, we put the captain in his stretcher over the side and into the water. Our only access to the water at this point was via the whaler's falls, which still hung vertically from the davit head. Shinning down, I paused on the lower block to take off my fur-lined boots before entering the water. I didn't get the chance as the 1st Lt. came down the fall on top of me and I found myself in the water. One of the signalmen who had been injured behind the wheelhouse was still in the water and asked me to help him. I saw him ashore all right and then began to realise the cold was colder than I had ever experienced before. By now, No4 gun had finished firing but the Germans were still firing at us, and bits of and pieces came flying over calling for numerous 'ducks' under the water in an effort to dodge the danger. The 1st Lt. was now calling for help with the chief stoker, so I went to give him a hand ashore. I then went back to assist the gunner (Mr McCracken) to bring the captain to the beach where he almost immediately died. I daresay he would have been happier had he known anything about it, if we had left him onboard.

My first wish now was to get the circulation going again, so I stamped my way up through the snow to the nearest house, as had so many others of our crew. Looking back, as I left the beach, I saw a ship upturned showing her keel, rudder and propellers, and felt that it must be one of the German destroyers that we had sunk. Unfortunately it turned out to be the 'Hunter', though I didn't know it at the time. Our own ship was on fire forward and rounds of ammunition of different calibres were exploding all the time.

I eventually reached the wooden house and there were two women there, a Mrs Christianson and her daughter, doing all they could to make the survivors comfortable. The house was full of steam from thawing bodies. Personally I was so cold and so exhausted that I could not take my soaking clothes off, though I knew I had to. A Yeoman of signals helped me out of them eventually and I wrapped myself in a black silk dress, which I found on the floor. I was glad now that that I had been unable to discard my boots at the bottom of the whalers fall when leaving the ship, for unlike most of the others I still had something to wear on my feet. Many made improvised shoes by cutting their rubber life jackets up and putting their feet in the two sealed ends. The most comical of all I think was our canteen manager who wrapped his legs around with newspaper. Then there was one who cut a hole in a carpet, put his head through it and tied the two draping ends around his body with a piece of string!

While I was still getting warm our torpedo officer called for volunteers to go back to the ship to get a man seen walking on the quarter deck. They went, four of them in a Carley float and brought back the navigator, for it was him…still in a concussed state. These four men were awarded the DSM and well deserved in view of the danger from exploding ammunition from the fires still raging onboard.

At about 1300 we made a move down the road away from Narvik. We were treated with many kindnesses by the Norwegians who gave us food and clothing etc. Eventually, at about 1900 we reached a village called Ballangen, where they opened a big centrally heated school for us and gave us tea, rye bread and some sausages to eat. It didn't take us long to get off to sleep that night, but it took a bit more effort to get us up the next morning. All that day the people of the village were bringing up bedding, clothes and food. They treated us well and the only way we could help them by way of payment was to give a hand at clearing away snow, which we all willingly did. During the day we visited the wounded in the hospital and they were as glad to see us, as we were to see them. We could all now find time enough to spare a moment or two for those, some of whom were very close friends, who were not just lucky enough to share our good fortune to have survived the battle of yesterday.

We stayed in Ballangen until the day of the second battle of Narvik. This was on Saturday April the 13th. This battle we were able to see from the attic of the school, and it was a grand sight to see the Tribal class destroyers driving Jerry step by step back up the fiord, with the battle ship 'Warspite' bringing up the rear and sending over salvo after salvo up the fiord, which must have had a great demoralising effect on the German destroyer crews. The torpedo officer Lt. Heppel put out in a local boat to try and contact one of our ships and on the way picked up a deserted German motor launch. This he took over to continue his mission. In the meantime the British ships continued to move up the fiord and out of our vision but we could hear the noise of battle as gunfire echoed and re echoed throughout the fiords. Lt Heppel made contact with the 'Ivanhoe', which very shortly came into Ballangen pier and took us off, and at the same time landed an armed guard to look after our wounded in the hospital.

The next morning we were transferred to different ships and I went on board the 'Hero', which was soon on the move down the fiord to the open sea. Orders were then received to join with 'Warspite' in patrolling an area, which we thought to be in the vicinity of the entrance to the fiord. We remained in this area with 'Warspite' until Thursday...nothing by way of excitement happened during that time. On Thursday we were told to sail for Rosyth, which pleased us no end. On the next evening, Friday, we heard on the news that the survivors of the 'Hardy' were arriving in London at any minute now, but obviously not our little group!....here we were, still out in the middle of the North Sea somewhere. Just twenty minutes later after this announcement the 'Hero' turned about and once more made a heading for the Narvik area, where we arrived on Sunday the 21st April in the afternoon. I can't express how we felt, but anyone who reads this may well imagine. Hardly had we dropped anchor than along came three German planes and dropped bombs. Fifteen minutes later, back they came to drop more, and shortly after this was followed by yet more attacks. No damage was suffered in any of the raids.

That same night we, the 'Hardy' survivors, were transferred to the troopship 'Franconia' which also re-embarked six hundred troops, whom it seemed she had transported to Norway earlier. We sailed again for home at 0800 on Tuesday the 23rd April. We had one escort for a little way and then was left to proceed on our own. All went well until 0200 on Friday morning when we were all awakened by a terrific explosion. I just stood there in the cabin, and well, I was quite surprised when the ship didn't heel over, or feel as though she may be sinking. We made our way up toward the upper deck but were stopped by the master at arms, who was saying that an escort had met us during the night and they were dropping depth charges. The explanation sounded feasible, so we made our way back down to our bunks and sleep again. The next morning the captain passed a message to us all, saying that during the night we had been attacked by torpedoes from a submarine and that they had exploded either in the ships wake, or at the end of their run. The next morning, Saturday the 27th we arrived safely back in Greenock and were soon on our way to Plymouth. Then the barrack staff re-kitted, paid and generally processed us, so that I was home on leave by 2000hrs on the Sunday, much to the relief of my family, who were really without word of our well being since the events of the 10th and the first battle of Narvik. The people of my village of Stoke Canon (*Four miles from Exeter*) gave me a great welcome home and presented me with a gold watch engraved as follows; Presented to Leslie J. Smale as an appreciation of services rendered on HMS Hardy at Narvik, 10th April 1940 by friends at Stoke Canon. In addition to this, they used the balance of the village collection to buy five War Savings certificates in my name."

Some of 'Hardy's Suicide Squad' in good spirits; they have survived.

The villagers make the presentation to Les. His family are present and behind him and to his right is Barbara his future wife.

Captain Bernard Warburton-Lee was awarded a posthumous Victoria Cross for his actions on the 10th at Narvik. The Admiralty had left it up to him to take action as he saw fit and it was his decision, and in the best traditions of the Royal Navy, to take the fight to the enemy. The loss of five large destroyers and other vessels at Narvik crippled future German actions at sea.

The graves in Ballangen of Cpt, Warburton Lee and some of those from Hardy and Hunter. (Commonwealth War Graves Comm.)

Operation Wilfred

Germany imported over 40 % of her iron ore, some 9m tons from Sweden. During the summer months it was via Lulea in the Gulf of Bothnia and the Baltic Sea. Lulea became ice bound during the winter months and the ore was transported by train to the ice free port of Narvik in Northern Norway. Ships were able to travel south from Narvik by way of a deep-water passage, within Norwegian territorial waters, known as the Indreled, or Inner Leads. It was also being used by blockade-runners, proceeding to and from the outer oceans for about a thousand miles; therefore they had the protection of Norwegian neutrality.

Churchill, as First Lord of the Admiralty had long advocated mining what he described as the Covered Way, in order to force enemy ships out of neutral waters where they could be intercepted.

The Royal Navy's 'H' class destroyers, completed in

1936, had a displacement of 1,340 tons. They had a main armament of four single 4.7" guns; the 'Hardy' had five. The German destroyers were much larger at over 2,000 tons and had five 5.9" guns, almost as big as a WWII cruiser.

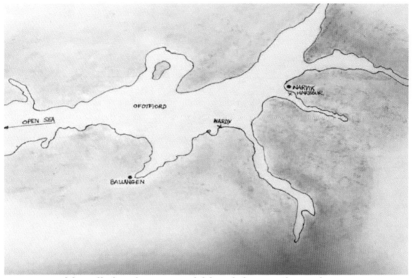

Narvik harbour and Hardy's resting place

DEMs GUNNER

JOHN DENIS ADDISON

IN AN OPEN BOAT

Den manning a 20mm Oerlikon anti-aircraft gun

John Denis Addison, known as Den, was born in 1913 and hailed from Ilkeston, Derbyshire. He joined the Royal Navy and trained as a seaman gunner. Two years later he was drafted to a merchant ship as a DEMs gunner (Defensively Equipped Merchant Ship). In the notes that he left he did not give the name of the merchant ship because at that time for security reasons he knew it would not get past the censor. The Royal Navy did not record the name of merchant ships on a man's personal file which also makes it difficult to identify it.

Quarters gunners badge. (Quarters = gun crew as opposed to control.)

He found himself on a merchant ship which sailed from England and would be heading for America, they would be sailing alone, not in convoy and for this reason their route would take them across the South Atlantic. By doing so they would hopefully avoid the U-boats prowling the North Atlantic routes. They had left the African coast behind and were about 600 miles west of Liberia and had almost reached the equator, Den was off watch and about to go below for his tot of rum and his dinner when there was a huge explosion and the front end of the ship heaved up out of the water. A torpedo had struck the ship in the bow. Apparently the look out on watch had seen its track coming but did not have time to warn the officer of the watch who may have been able to take avoiding action. Den started to make his way towards his action station, which was a gun on the stern of the ship, but before he got there another torpedo struck amidships. This one threw him up in the air and he landed on the deck winded and in shock for a few seconds. Bits of debris were falling all around him, but he eventually managed to gather his wits and make his way to his action station. The leading seaman had already arrived at the gun and he told Den to go back as there was nothing to shoot at and they were abandoning ship, he had not heard the order to abandon ship and must have been temporarily unconscious.

Torpedoed, a DEMs manned ship, a gun can be seen on the stern.

As he made his way forward, he came across a mate who had been hit on the head by some wreckage and was concussed. He helped him up and they went forward together. There were four lifeboats onboard, two they found had already been launched and the explosion had wrecked a third. The Captain was still aboard with about six others and together they launched the fourth boat. As this boat was being launched it capsized and the men were tipped into the water. Den's gunner mate went under and he did not see him surface again. With difficulty they managed to right the boat and get back into it. However, they could not get away, the boat was being held alongside the ship, and the ship was still going slowly ahead. Despite the fact that the ship was starting to sink the propeller was still turning. Den again looked around for his 'oppo' but could not see him; they had seen sharks in the water earlier in the day or it may be that he'd been drawn into the propeller.!

The boat slowly slid towards the stern along the side of the ship and it just missed the thrashing prop. A short while after the ship went down the U-boat surfaced about four hundred yards from them.

It came towards the lifeboat that Den was in and in perfect English a German officer hailed them asking if the ships captain was in the boat. Somebody said 'Yes' and the captain stood up and identified himself. He was told to get onto the submarine 'peacefully' or else... It was difficult for him to board it because of the swell and the bulge of the submarines side, but having boarded it he was put below. The U-boat captain asked where we were going and shouted 'Good Luck' before submerging and disappearing.

Just North of the equator and 1200 miles to go. A very sobering experience, stranded in an open boat hundreds of miles from land.

Each boat had a small compass and after a conference they decided, because of the prevailing tides and winds it would be easier to go the estimated 1,200 miles towards Brazil than to fight the currents and winds going back the estimated 600 miles to South Africa.

They hoisted some sails and agreed to set one-hour watches between them. Luckily, the weather was good, and a reasonable sea was running. One thing bothered them was the fact that a lot of sharks were swimming round, they could feel them sometimes bumping the bottom of the boat. Towards the end of that afternoon, they started to take stock of the rations available. There were the emergency rations that were always kept in lifeboats, two large, sealed tins of ships biscuits, two small barrels of fresh water, twelve tins of corned beef and twelve tins of milk. It was a bit of a shock on opening the first tin of biscuits to find they had had gone mouldy.

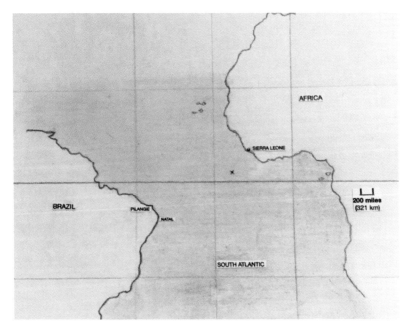

From Sierra Leone/Liberia to Brazil = 1879 miles (3024km)

Thankfully the second tin was okay. Their tea that evening consisted of one hard tack biscuit and two ounces of water each... worse than prison rations?

Nothing much happened for a couple of monotonous days; we mainly sat looking at each other and not much was said! After a spell of rough weather, the tiller broke on his boat and it became waterlogged and was in danger of sinking. Again, luck was with Den as the three boats had managed to stay together for two days. Three men went into each of the other two boats. They took anything of use from their boat and

divided what rations they had between the two remaining boats. They then cast the other boat adrift. If the boats had separated in the bad weather, they would not have survived.
On the third night the two boats got separated, as the other boat was a knot or two sailing faster than Den's.

They spoke to each other less and less as time went on. Sharks were swimming around and constantly bumping the boat. They were concerned that their compass was not very reliable, and they may not make land and, because they were not on a regular shipping lane they may not get picked up. During the night it was bitterly cold and during the day it was blistering hot. Being in the tropics the only clothing they had on when abandoning ship was a pair of shorts each so during the day, they took it in turns to sit in the shadow of the sail. They began to run short of water so when on the fifth day it began to rain, they thought their luck was in. They lowered the sail and caught about two gallons of water in it... imagine their disappointment when they found the preserving chemicals in the canvas had contaminated the water to such an extent it was bitter and undrinkable.

After a week in the boat there was a thunderstorm when they were able to catch some more water in the sail, which was just drinkable now that the first rains had washed it. They all drank their fill and there was still enough to top up one of the barrels. There were shoals of fish and dolphins from time to time around the boat and a few flying fish came inboard. Anything they got their hands on was eaten there and then uncooked or kept for later.

They were continually bailing water from the boat and they took turns doing it. One night their hopes were raised when some way off a plane flew over. They lit six flares to attract attention, but the plane flew on. The following day they saw four more aircraft in the distance but could not get their attention either. However, they were cheered up to know they must now have a better chance of making a landfall.

A couple of nights later Den was on watch in the bow and apart from the man on the tiller everyone else was asleep. He thought he could see a very dim light way out on the horizon, but he dared not say anything in case it was his imagination. Half an hour later he could still see it and he shouted out 'Lights ahead'. They decided it was a land-based navigation light for shipping and they dared to get excited. One of the officers in the boat suddenly produced a bottle of cognac, which he said he had been saving for 'medicinal purposes'! They all celebrated with a good drink of extra water and a double dose of cognac. From then on nobody could sleep that night but stayed up watching the light all night... just in case it went away!

The following morning, after nearly three weeks in the boat they could just make out a vague outline of what looked like land. During the day the land took on a definite outline, they now knew they had a good chance of surviving, this became reality when they saw in the distance a small fishing boat with what turned out to be four Brazilian fishermen in it. One of Den's merchant crewmen who could speak passable Portuguese was able to converse with them, he learned that they came from a small village of just a few huts they called Pilangie. The nearest town was Natal, Brazil; this they said was about 20 miles away. As they neared the beach, they could not see any houses but on getting closer they spied a few native huts amongst the palms. Later that day they landed on a sandy beach and got out of the boat, they could hardly stand after nearly three weeks cramped in the open boat. With the help of the natives, they managed to crawl up under the shade of the palm trees.

There were about two hundred people in the village and they luckily all turned out to be very friendly toward them. Some of the natives climbed the palms and cut down coconuts for the survivors to drink and eat.

The headman of the group was eventually made to understand that we needed to get a message through to the authorities that they had survived and needed to make contact. The chief explained that it would take some time, as the only means of transport was a donkey. However, one of the fit young natives volunteered to run to the nearest town with a message. One was written explaining who they were and that they needed help.

That night they were fed more fruit and fish and were entertained for the evening. The natives put on a pretty decent show with various singers and acrobatics.

Later the next day what was to turn out to be a Brazilian submarine chaser was seen out at sea. They made their location known by signalling to them and the warship came inshore as far as it could without grounding. Eventually the natives took them out to the ship in their boats and they were hauled aboard. Onboard the warship they were given a good meal and were taken to Natal where the British consul was waiting for them. He took charge of their welfare and removed them to the Police hospital. There they were examined and most of them were found to be in pretty good shape, although there were three or four who were not. They were suffering mainly from chest and lung problems due to fuel ingestion and exposure and one subsequently died from heart failure. So near yet so far...

Those who were well enough were supplied with tropical clothing and sent to a hotel. They languished there in this strange place for five wonderful weeks until Den received a telegram to say that there would be a British mine sweeper in the harbour at Pernambuco and he was to join her there. He was to leave the merchant crew there and was to board an American transport plane to get there.

His return to England was not entirely uneventful. The ship he was on was escorting a homeward convoy which was attacked by enemy aircraft. He saw at least three enemy planes shot down.

They arrived in the UK, the port was not named because of the censor, and Den finally got survivors leave. After all he'd been through, he arrived home in Ilkeston, to find that his parents, Martha and John, had been bombed out of their house on the 5th September 1940 and had moved to 9, Kingsway and that his brother Thomas had joined the army. (Kingsway was also later bombed in 1942).

Den's parents home at 367 Nottingham Road had been bombed. Luckily the occupants of these houses had just been evacuated because of a previously unexploded bomb so nobody was killed. (Sarah Munro)

Den was typical of many Royal Navy men; he was very proud of his service and was 'Once Navy, always Navy'. Like many survivors they didn't talk about it much. Most of them loved a drink, probably helped them to forget the trauma they had suffered. Den was always life and sole of a party, his party piece being the sailor's hornpipe, which he could dance and sing from beginning to end.

It was said that the captain of his ship, who was taken aboard the submarine was never heard of again, it transpired that the U-boat was attacked and only a few of the crew survived. There were so many ships torpedoed in the South Atlantic that its difficult to identify the ship that Den was on.

Such is fate!

RIP
John Denis Addison RN

ESCAPE FROM BOULOGNE

HECTOR FRANK KNELL

PRIVATE 6347125

ROYAL WEST KENT REGIMENT

Hector (author)

In 1939 life was good for Hector, he was a young man working at Wick's bakery at Tongue Mill near Sittingbourne, Kent. Mr Wicks taught him to drive in order that he could make the rural bread deliveries. He had met a young girl, Jesse Quested, on his rounds. WWII intervened and on the 16th August 1939 Hector received his call up papers to join the army. He was to report to the historical Blandford barracks at Pimperne in Dorset on the 16th October. After his initial training he joined the 6/7th Royal West Kent Regiment based at Invicta Park barracks Maidstone. They were nicknamed 'The blind half hundred' or

'The dirty half hundred'! As he already had a driving licence, which was not that common then, he was assigned as a transport driver. The war had started the previous month and his regiment was to be sent to France with the British Expeditionary Force.

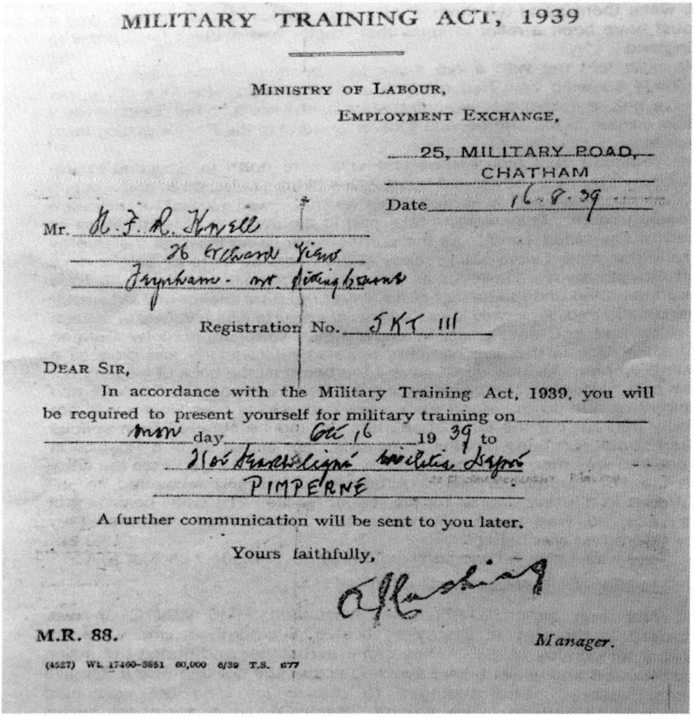

MILITARY TRAINING ACT, 1939

MINISTRY OF LABOUR,

EMPLOYMENT EXCHANGE,

25, MILITARY ROAD,
CHATHAM

Date _16·8·39_

Mr. _H. J. R. Knell_

76 Orchard View

Frynham · nr. Gillingham

Registration No. _SKT III_

DEAR SIR,

In accordance with the Military Training Act, 1939, you will be required to present yourself for military training on _____

Mon day _Oct 16_ 19 _39_ to

No Transceiving Militia Depot

PIMPERNE

A further communication will be sent to you later.

Yours faithfully,

A Hocking

M.R. 88.

(4527) Wt. 17460-3851 60,000 6/39 T.S. 677   *Manager.*

Hectors call up papers

36

Kings Own Royal West Kent Regimental badge. (author)

in an attempt to halt the German invasion of Europe. He and Jessie married in March 1940 and within days his regiment left Southampton aboard channel ferries, amongst them the 'Isle of Man' and 'Lady of Man'. Their regiment formed a part of the 36th Brigade, which also consisted of the 5th Battalion the East Kent Regiment, or the 'Buffs'.

They arrived in Le Havre and berthed alongside the burnt-out wreck of the huge liner 'Paris'. Disembarking they drove in convoy to a small village about twelve miles the other side of Rouen.

For a couple of months, he was involved in moving ammunition and barbed wire from a huge dump near Rouen to the front, taking troops to and from Pont de Larche and Louviers and various other tasks. He was enjoying France in the spring with fine warm weather; he said they could swim in nearby lakes, watched by the locals. Then one day in May they heard a rumour that some German tanks had broken through the line but that they were being rounded up. The following day they were loading some barbed wire onto their vehicles from the dump when a bugle sounded the emergency stand to. They quickly emptied their lorries and returned to the camp. All troops were to be embarked and load as much of the stores as they could, then destroy anything of use to the enemy. They were ordered into convoy and drove off towards the north east.

The officers in charge knew what was happening but most of the men at that time did not have much idea where they were going. They drove all night and at times found it difficult getting through the crowds of French refugees fleeing ahead of them. There were times when they not only had Germans behind them but in front of them as well. What he probably did not know at the time was that the whole of the German 6th Panzer (tank) Brigade was over running their position. Although Royal West Kents and the Buffs were only infantry they actually slowed the German tanks advance by destroying various strategic bridges and river crossings and destroyed several of the tanks in the process.

Cut off from Dunkirk Hector drove for Boulogne.

They were ordered to the town of Doullens, about 15 miles north of Amiens, arriving on the 19th May and made ready to make a stand and to defend the town.

Brigadier Rouple had told his officers that if and when the time came, they were to escape with their troops north towards Frevent. The time then came with news of a disastrous battle at Albert and then they themselves came under intense artillery and machine gun fire. About a hundred troops were left as a rearguard and after making a stand were eventually captured. Brigadier Rouple escaped and hid in a barn for two years, finally escaping through Spain. Several lorry loads of troops were ordered to make their escape from Doullens, Hector amongst them, driving his lorry they managed to cross the Somme.

It was during the night convoy from Rouen to Doullens that Hector said something happened to change his life. The driver of the lorry in front of him was wandering all over the road presumably falling asleep at the wheel. When they next stopped for a break and a drink an officer came back to Hector and asked him if they had an NCO onboard, Hector said that he did not know. The officer said I will be travelling with you from here on because if we stay with the guy in front, he's falling asleep at the wheel and he'll kill us all.

Hector died before he was able to finish writing his story. However from what I remember him telling me and from the official history of the regiment it transpired that because he was driving the officer in question, he escaped being captured at Doullens, if he hadn't been driving him he could very well have been left there to be captured or killed.

They had been ordered to fall back to Dunkirk but had been cut off and were unable to do so, they made for Boulogne docks. I recall him telling me that as they drove into Boulogne with the Germans chasing them down the road, he saw another column of Germans crossing the road some way ahead of them. He quickly turned around and in doing so his back wheels dropped into a ditch. He revved the engine until the truck was jumped out of the ditch by the men in the back. He drove round the back of the town and made for the docks. On arrival there he shouted to the men in the lorry that it was now; 'Every man for himself'. They pushed the lorry in to the sea to wreck it and they all ran towards a couple of Royal Navy destroyers that were alongside the dock.   These two destroyers, HMS Wild Swan and her sister ship, were the last ones to leave from Boulogne. The ships were not made fast to the dock but were being held there on their engines. He said he ran across a plank of wood, which was about to be thrown overboard.

The two ships went full astern out of the harbour whilst they were firing to great effect over open sights at the German tanks coming down the road, several of which were destroyed. There were huge explosions going on all around them as the demolitions were going off at the gasholders and petrol and ammunition dumps.

HMS Wild Swan

'Wild Swan' was bombed and strafed all the way back to Dover with many of the soldiers on the upper decks being injured. She had 1,400 men crammed in every available space between and on her decks, plus her normal compliment of 160 or so crew.   A near miss by the stern damaged one of the destroyers 'A' brackets and she finished the journey on one propeller. She later had to go up the Thames to Tilbury docks for repairs.

They arrived in Dover late at night where it was chaos, several ships were unloading thousands of troops. Hector managed to find a nearby shop owner who had a telephone, a fairly rare item in those days, and he was able to ring his old boss at Tonge Mill bakery near Sittingbourne, where he used to be a delivery driver. He asked him if he would inform his mother and father that he had made it back all right. Mr Wicks, the owner of the bakery, went to their house at 26 Orchard View, Teynham in the middle of the night, he threw lumps of dirt up to their window to wake them up to tell them that Hector had made it back from France and that he was O.K. At a very confused and worrying time it must have been a relief for them to know that Hector had made it back home to England.

Hector later told me with a wry smile that because of the confusion and nobody knowing who had made it and who hadn't, he took six weeks unofficial leave before reporting to his unit that he had made it home!

Life was good again for Hector and Jesse and their first son, David, was born in 1941. He was still in the army and in August they travelled to Scotland where they they underwent further training for landing operations. At the end of October, they were embarked on troopships. They did not know where they were going until they had sailed. The 6th Brigade were to be attached to the 78th 'Battleaxe' Division and be involved in Operation Torch, the invasion of North Africa. On the 8th November 42 they arrived at Safi near Algiers to disembark, it was a nerve wracking time because whilst unloading their vehicles from the ship, they were to remain in the cab, swinging from the end of a crane, in order to speed up the process, this while air attacks were expected! They were to join a convoy in the 'Run for Tunis'. He said at night you followed the vehicle in front of you by one small light on its' rear. On one occasion they were accidentally diverted onto the temporary runway of an airfield when a driver tried to follow the tail light of an aircraft taxiing to take off!

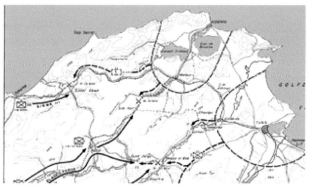
The Run for Tunis, the Djebel Abiod Road.

About the 17th August they were travelling along the Djebel Aliod – Mateur Road towards Tunis when they came under attack from the air by German Stuka dive bombers. His lorry was targetted and a bomb was dropped that landed under the tail gate of the lorry. It blew the vehicles rear end over its front and it landed upside down. Hector had to be pulled from under the cab, but luckily, he had only suffered cuts and bruises and was temporarily deafened. He'd escaped serious injury. However, he was shook up and suffered from quite serious 'shell shock', something he never got over for the rest of his life. He always had a nervous twitch and at times of stress his hands would shake. He was shipped home and given home leave. He was eventually discharged as unfit for further service on the 18th September 1943.

Discharged as unfit for further service.

He was awarded a small pension, but this was taken off him twelve months later 'because they considered he was better'! He had survived and was luckier than the many that never made it back at all!

Hectors War Medals

1939-40 Defence Medal. Africa Star.1939-45 Star.1939-45 War Medal

During the earlier rear guard action at Doullens in France, Private Alan Fisher of the Buffs was captured and interred as a POW in Germany and was, after nearly five years, repatriated after the war. Although he and Hector never met during the war, many years later Alan's daughter Madeleine, met and married Hector's nephew Roger, it's a small world.

On the 16th June 1942, HMS Wild Swan was escorting convoy HG84 in the Atlantic south of Ireland. She was passing a small fleet of Spanish fishing boats when twelve German bombers, who were looking for the convoy, came across 'Wild Swan' and mistook the Spanish boats for the convoy. 'Wild Swan' received four near misses which damaged her steering and out of control she collided with one of the fishing boats. She managed to save 11 of the Spanish crew and in the following action managed to shoot down 6 of the enemy aircraft. Very good shooting in the days before radar-controlled guns. She was badly damaged by the bombing and the collision with the fishing boat and finally sank. All the crew of 144 plus the 11 Spanish fishermen, successfully took to the lifeboats. They were picked up fifteen hours later by one of her sister ships. Unfortunately, 31of the crew had died from exposure. Such is fate.

NEVER FORGOTTEN

HMS BULLEN

JIM HALL

The frigate HMS Bullen.

WARNING - Not for the faint hearted!

What follows is the story, in his own words, of the torpedoing and sinking of HMS Bullen as seen through the eyes of Jim Hall, one of the survivors. His wife knew that he suffered from nightmares related to his wartime experience, but he never spoke of it. Three years after he 'Crossed the Bar' (*died*) his wife found the story he had written in a drawer. Be warned, a part of this story is horrific and not for the feint hearted.

"0900hrs the 6th of November 1944, somewhere in the North Sea, I could see the Isle of Skye and then it happened, HMS Bullen was hit by a torpedo, I was down in the paint locker with two or three of my mates. Bells were ringing there were no lights... they all went out. We scrambled out to the upper deck the best we could. We didn't know what had happened really till we got to the upper deck. Yes, she'd been hit amidships the deck was all buckled. Most people mainly ratings... didn't know what had happened really. We just looked dazed... I expect frightened. We were just young men it was the first time anything like this had happened to us. I always remember asking if they'd blow my life belt up for me, I don't think I'd got enough wind to blow it up. Anyway, it wasn't long before the captain gave the order to abandon ship.

I couldn't swim. I knew I couldn't. I couldn't pass the swimming test when I joined the navy. I was what they called a 'backward swimmer'. In fact they told me I would never swim but I would never go under. I was going to have to try it. I lowered myself over the side, I dropped onto a cork net, it hadn't been unwrapped and more men dropped onto it and it was going round and round and I kept going over and under. I didn't know what to do I thought well... If I keep hold of this I'm definitely going to go under, stuck in the middle of it. I thought well Jim... you've got to do something. You've either got to let go.... But I didn't, I climbed.... I got hold of a rope that was hanging from the ship and I let go of the cork net and climbed up back on board the ship.

When I got onboard I heard someone shouting I got to him the best way that I could, there was another rating there with me. One of the ratings was trying to get out of the deck... Ill never forget it... he was so far out he couldn't get past his stomach... they were steel decks and we were trying to prise the deck open to get to him.

All of a sudden the ship gave a lurch as if something was going to happen, and it did... it chopped this rating in two... I'd never seen anything like that before. I didn't know what I was doing but all I kept thinking was I've got to get away I've got to go.

I jumped over the side. I knew I couldn't swim there was no

cork net to stand on or get hold of so I drifted and drifted. I must have got far enough away, I kept looking back and half the ship had gone down. Ratings were still clinging to the bows of the ship. I didn't know what to think, it was snowing, raining, the sea was rough. It was winter wasn't it? I couldn't feel my legs or my hands. It was freezing, the water was icy. I always remember there was a flying boat flying over us, it kept coming down low. It must have been looking at us, watching us. We knew there were submarines about.

Other escort ships were dropping depth charges, that didn't make it any better. The flying boat came over low again, low. I remember trying to lift my arms up to get hold of the bottom of the aeroplane. It was no good, no good but I tried. I would have done if I could reach but no, it wasn't to be.

Swimmers kept passing me. They couldn't help anybody, they were too cold as well, and they couldn't do anything. It seemed that I just went on and on. I've never known anything like it. It seemed such a long time… it was a long time… before anyone came to help us. Escort ships were racing by, still dropping depth charges. That was the first priority I expect. They had to do that first, destroy the submarines, kill them. They did their best it seemed hours and hours. I know I was picked up by one of the whalers, a small boat. (*A destroyers boat*) They pulled me aboard and took me to one of the escort ships. I remember them pulling me up a rope.

When they got me on deck two men tried to stand me up but I couldn't. My legs and arms felt as if they were two feet wide. I expect it was frostbite. I can't remember any more. I was told that they took me to the Isle of Skye and put me on a hospital ship. I can't remember anything. I had been in the water for over three hours, perhaps a bit longer. I can't remember even seeing the hospital ship. They took me off and put me on the train the next day. When I came to I was in Crewe, passing Crewe station on the way to Chatham barracks. We were leaving Crewe I think I was just beginning to come round. I saw one or two of the lads on the train with me. We looked a mess. We were still covered in oil; I don't think they'd tried to get it off us. Everything we were dressed in was what our mates had given us. We were on our way to Chatham barracks and didn't know what we would find there. It seemed like hours on the train but at last we got to Chatham and they'd sent transport to the station to take us to the barracks. I was still cold. I didn't think I would ever get warm again. It was winter. They took us to the gymnasium and we slept on the floor on hammocks all night after we'd had hot drinks. I don't think anybody wanted to eat. I don't think we could. The next morning we had hot baths but we still couldn't get clean. They gave us uniforms; I don't think they fitted properly. We were given money to go home, that meant another train journey but still, we were going home.

My parents had received a telegram from the admiralty stating that I was missing and then another informing them that I was safe. I can't remember what they said to me when I got home. I think all I wanted to do was get in the bath. A day or two later my brother got married and I was best man. I can't remember much more about that. We had a fortnights leave and I was under the doctor strait away. As soon as my leave had finished I had to make my way back. They'd had a letter from my doctor telling them about my condition so I was actually put on light duties.

We slept in tunnels underground because of the air raids everyone from the barracks slept underground. It was after a couple of days that the Royal Navy police were waking me up asking me to get out of my hammock. I will always remember it. There was only my hammock strung up in the tunnels. I tried but couldn't get out. Finally they lifted me out, took my hammock down, dressed me and took me to the mess. I had a wash and drink and I was sent, well they took me, to see the doctor. I still had the police with me and they took me to the station and got on the train with me. I ended up in Cheshire.

They sent me to a place called Chumleigh Castle, and it was a castle, an old one. They were all sailors there who'd been shipwrecked at some time or other.

Chalmondley Castle.

The doctors were all psychiatrists. It was a queer place, very queer. We used to see the doctors every day and we did little chores anything to keep us busy. The doctors kept talking to us, everything was written down. I stayed there for six months. I knew there was something wrong with me; I kept having nightmares, bad dreams. After six months they let me go home for a spot of leave. But I was never the same again; I couldn't forget what I'd gone through.

I finally got on a ship, on a cruiser, but it wasn't the same I just couldn't rest. I came off that and they sent me on an aircraft carrier. Whilst I was on the carrier my demob number came up. I was going home for good, out of the navy.

Forty-eight years later, I read an advert in one of the local papers. One of my shipmates was asking about me, he wanted to know if I was all right. He came from London, Steve

----- and he invited me to his home so I went to see him. He was waiting at the station for me and I stayed with him for two or three days. It was marvellous; it had been a long time. He wrote me when I got home and he said he'd like to start to have a reunion with some of the lads. He'd contacted some of them and felt that we should all meet. So we've now had about seven reunions and they've been really marvellous, some of our friends we've missed and some we've enjoyed meeting. At the last reunion that I went to I met a man who had tried to help me get that sailor out of the ship. He knew me straight away; he knew who I was and he asked me if I remembered. I told him that I would never forget. To think that I had abandoned ship and gone back on again... abandoning the same ship twice. I still have these bad turns so many years afterwards. Sometimes I wake up in the night and I don't know where I am or I'm onboard ship and it happens again. I expect I will always have them but I'll never forget, I'll never forget that day, it was a very bad day, everyone says the same. I still like to meet my shipmates although there are few of us left. It was reported that the submarine was blown to the surface by depth charges the following day. They surrendered to naval forces and were interned. The submarine was taken out to sea and sunk by gunfire. I did meet one of the crew at one of our reunions, but I couldn't talk to him, I don't think I wanted to".

Fate?

Most people would not have survived more than 15 to 20 minutes in the freezing waters at that time of the year.
It's very easy to get confused at a time of stress but it would appear that 'Bullen' as said was actually about 7 miles North West of Cape Wrath which would put her in the North Atlantic ocean not the North Sea, and in that case the island he saw was probably the Isle of Lewis rather than the Isle of Skye.

Chumleigh or Chumley Castle, were the colloquial names for Chalmondeley Castle in Cheshire. It was requisitioned during WWII as a Royal Naval Auxiliary hospital.

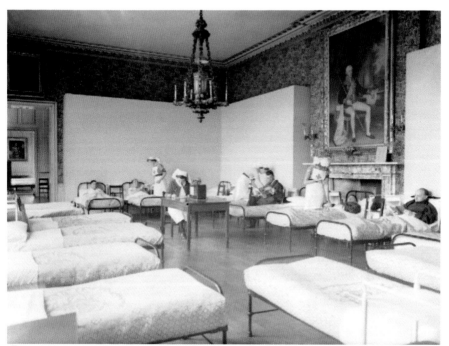

Royal Navy Auxiliary nurses in the ward in Chalmondeley Castle WWII. It is tempting to think that one of these patients could very well have been Jim Hall or his shipmates. (H. W. Tomkin RN photographer)

HMS Bullen was a lend lease destroyer from the USA but was classified by the Royal Navy as a Frigate. She was attached to the 19th Escort Group but did not survive long. She was torpedoed and sunk by U-775, 7 miles off Cape Wrath at 58.43' N – 004.51', off the West coast of Scotland. U-775 was said to have been sunk the following day. But she actually survived till the end of the war. She surrendered in 1945 at Trondheim, Norway. Sometimes information was given out that probably made the survivors feel better thinking that retribution had been exacted, it may just have been rumour or that the true facts were not made available till after the war.

Lt. Cdr. Parish, the 'Bullen's' captain perished in the sinking along with 71 others of her crew. Jim and the rest of the survivors were picked up by the destroyers HMS Goodall and Hesperus.

Jim's wife passed his story to Vic Ould, a wartime served naval rating, who had already written a book on the loss of the 'Bullen'. He passed the story on to me when he visited the Destroyer memorial at Chatham Historic Dockyard.

HMS MEDWAY

M.E. CYRIL DAVIS RN

Dave Davis (Linda Davis)

Dave was born Cyril Davis but was known by all as David or Dave. He was born in Teynham Kent in 1921 and joined the Royal Navy in 1939, training as an engine room stoker, first at Skegness for his initial training and then HMS Pembroke at Chatham.

In 1940 he was drafted to his first ship, the flower class corvette HMS Primula (K14). It was on this ship that he experienced his first brush with danger, and it was his first lucky escape. They were escorting a convoy to Russia when one afternoon, having had the middle watch, he was dozing on a mess bench when there was an almighty crash. He awoke to see the bow of a huge merchant ship which had collided with his ship and crashed through the ships side just a few feet away from him. Luckily most of the damage was above the water line and there was no immediate danger of 'Primula' sinking. Having shored up the damage she spent two rough days getting back to England. She went straight up the Thames to the Royal Albert Dock for repairs. This was handy for Dave as he lived at Sittingbourne and was able to get some home leave.

In 1942 he volunteered for service in submarines (probably thought it was safer under the water than on it!) and underwent specialist training at HMS Dolphin in Portsmouth. Here he learnt all about a submariner's life and was taught how to escape from a sunken submarine. He trained on the escape apparatus in the 30 metre (100ft) deep tank of water.... not for the faint hearted! Later in 1942 he was drafted to the submarine depot ship HMS Medway (F25) as spare submarine crew for the 1st Submarine Flotilla based in the Mediterranean. 'Medway' had been based in Alexander, Egypt since April 1940. The Mediterranean was a dangerous place for submarines, because of the shallow water they could quite easily be seen from the air. Medway was a large ship at 14,650 tons and in war time could be 'mother' to 21 submarines. The submarine crews would live onboard in relative comfort when returning from patrol. As spare crew and having rested, they would then take another submarine out, it having been serviced, refuelled, stocked with food and torpedoes and ammunition from 'mother'.

HMS Medway submarine depot ship

Dave did a couple of patrols on HMS Thunderbolt (N25). '
Thunderbolt' was the salvaged and renamed HMS
Thetis, tragically sunk on her trials in Liverpool Bay in 1938.
Ninety nine men, plus one of the salvage team lost their lives.
In her time in the Mediterranean, she was credited with sinking
ten or more enemy ships. She was also fitted to carry Chariots
(Human Torpedoes). Once again Dave was lucky because
having left her, she was lost on her next patrol in Cape San Vito
Bay off Sicily, there were no survivors.

HMSM Thunderbolt leaving for a patrol, HMS Medway left background.

In June 1942 it was feared that Rommel's Panza army
was about to overrun the port of Alexander and attack Egypt.
Therefore, Vice Admiral Harwood, C in C Mediterranean,
ordered all ships in the port of Alexander to leave and sail for
Beirut, where they were to set up a new base. 'Medway'
loaded all the stores she could, including 1,135 personnel from
the base, including some WRENs and at 0815hrs on the 30th
June she sailed. She was escorted by the Cruiser 'Dido', seven
destroyers and accompanied by the Greek SS Corinthia.
Having sailed and reached a point just off Port Said,
Dave had come off watch and had gone for a shower, he had

just got in there when there were three huge and deafening explosions, and the ship was lifted almost out of the water. Dave was thrown to the deck. The ship took on an immediate and alarming list to port. The Germans had received information that she was sailing and U-Boat 372, Cdr. Heinz–Joachim Newmann, had been waiting for her. Dave and a friend who had also been in the showers, made a dash for the upper deck... with no clothes on! They were running along a passageway when several heavy 45-gallon drums broke loose, one of which struck Dave in the face and knocked him to the deck. He didn't know how but he struggled to the upper deck and because it was such a long drop over the side, his friend shouted to him to say there was a rope hanging over the side, his mate grabbed the rope and jumped but the rope was not tied to anything and he fell. Dave remembers being in the sea for about an hour or more and then grabbing a scrambling net hung over the side of the destroyer HMS 'Pakenham'. He thinks he must have been unconscious at some stage because the next thing he remembers is waking up and seeing a WREN standing over his naked body! Thirty of 'Medway's' crew were killed but mercifully most of the passengers were rescued by the escorting destroyers. Later 47 of the 90 expensive torpedoes onboard 'Medway' floated to the surface and were salvaged. 'Pakenham' took some of the survivors to Port Said where in the hospital it was found that Dave had three fractures to his jaw where the oil drum had hit him. His jaw was wired up with nuts and bolts which every now and again were tightened to pull his jaw back into shape. A tooth that was missing allowed him to suck water and soup through a straw! After several weeks he was shipped out and was to go via the Cape in Africa for what he thought would be some welcome survivors leave back in England. However, it was not to be, they arrived in South Africa and were disembarked into canvas tents at Peitermaritzberg. He was to spend nearly a year there before finally being repatriated...he said he left a son there who he never met! He served the rest of the war without incident and having completed his twelve years retired from the service in 1951.

'Medway' lies in the Mediterranean at 32' 03"N by 34' 37"E.'

Dave was active till the end, he belonged to the Sittingbourne Royal Navy Association, loved a beer every weekend and line dancing. He lived to almost to 100yrs old... Fate?

HMS DELIGHT

G. LAWRENCE Padre

NURSE DOREEN HOLNESS

Nurse Doreen Holness, King's College Hospital 1939 (Author)

HMS Delight, pennant number H38, had recently returned from the China station and had just completed a refit in Britain. On the 31st July 1940 at about 1830hrs she was steaming at 23 knots in a calm sea and approaching the tidal races off Portland Bill off Dorset, when there was an explosion alongside and several more were heard by the those below, men rushed up to get to their action stations when another explosion blew several of them onto their backs. Recovering they ran to the bridge where there had been a near miss, all the armoured glass was shattered and splinter holes were everywhere; everyone on the bridge was in a state of shock but did not appear to be seriously injured, although it was later found that the Captain had received a splinter wound which had penetrated his chest. The ship had come to a standstill.

On the torpedo men's mess deck there was a fire and the damage control party had rigged hoses to fight it, even although the mess was full of acrid smoke and all the lights had gone out.

In the next compartment, the low power room, there was a raging fire; it was so hot nobody could enter it. Splinters from the bomb had killed the duty switchboard operator and his body was in the fire unable to be reached. Several technical personnel had also been killed or injured; in fact, only one of the five Electrical Artificers had not been killed or injured by the initial blast as well as many other key personnel who could have helped in fighting the fires. (*Later in the war it became standard for ships crews to be organised so that half of each branch were forward and the others aft so that some of each branch would survive to run the ship in this event*). The fires in the mess decks and power room then spread to the fuel tanks below, it was realized that the main ammunition magazine would be next and if the ship was not to blow up this had to be flooded. This was done with difficulty because the connecting pipes could not be found. Eventually a jury rig was cobbled together, and water was got into the magazine. (*Another lesson learned from this for the future was to have valves on the upper deck which enabled the magazine to be flooded from there.*)

Another known danger was the ready use ammunition that was kept in lockers by the guns; the guns crew and ammunition suppliers did their job properly and were rapidly ditching it all over the side.

A 'D' class destroyer, HMS Delight lies in two parts on the seabed off Portland in Dorset, she is a protected war grave.

This was to prevent further explosions if the fire should spread to that area.

The Petty officer telegraphist who had been badly injured was nevertheless attempting to raise the alarm and get help from ashore; the ratings in his charge were dumping all the secret codes over the side in weighted bags. Several fires were burning around the bridge and the machine gun ammunition was exploding like fireworks. A three badge Able seaman, Richard 'Rattler' Morgan had lost a leg and died later. Someone gave permission for rum to be issued whilst we awaited rescue and a cup was passed round. Shortly afterwards several small harbour craft arrived from Portland and several aircraft arrived over us, at first it was thought they might be the enemy returning to finish us however they turned out to be friendly. After the injured had been placed in the boats and everyone else had been got off the ship it was decided she could not be saved and should be sunk. A small minelayer ran in several times under her bow and dropped several depth charges set shallow to scuttle her.

On arrival ashore the injured were placed on stretchers and transferred to hospital. One of these was the ships Writer, Shepherd, who was in fact not injured but had had too much medicinal rum and someone on one of the boats had supplied whiskey as well!

The unwounded ratings were taken to the barracks and the officers due to lack of space there for them, were taken to the Salvation Army quarters.

Twenty-one men were killed and many injured. Some of the more seriously injured were taken to specialist hospitals in London for treatment. Miss Doreen Holness, a nursing sister at Kings College Hospital, remembers treating many of them. This must have been something of a shock for a young girl thrown into treating war wounded. She later kept up a correspondence with one of 'Delight's' survivors who later reported the actions he was involved in on another destroyer in the Mediterranean. He was unable to say what ship he was on because of the censor but kept a running commentary on what they were involved in. It's possible now to work out what ship this would have been. C. Lawrence in fact was a padre and was on HMS Faulkner attached to force 'H'. Part of one of his letters is transcribed below:

My Dears All

Please forgive the long delay in answering your grand letter – actually four months ago – much has happened to all of us since that time & I do hope you are all well & truly happy – as happy as is possible under the circumstances.
You will never know the inspiration you who are carrying on in London & all other places that are being bombed, are to those in the fighting forces – especially to those in the Navy – everyone of us have remarked how we were absolutely scared stiff on the occasions when we were in houses during a raid – I

know I was & was thankful to be back in the comparative safety of the ship.

At least we can keep our nautical home moving about & stick our porcupine quills up when the wicked enemy is about!

As you have been hearing on the news we have been having some real fun & games with the Italians in the Mediterranean - they have let us have things our own way – although now that the Jerries are stiffening them up we have had to be more careful.

The scrap off Sardinia was rather like an exciting film show, seen from a destroyer in between the main units it was more like watching the show being filmed and helping in the noise effects - & if ever we have a chance I have some grand photographs to show you all.

Today we had some luck we picked up a very small boat miles out in the Atlantic with four men in it that had been drifting about since Dec 23rd they were amazingly fit considering their ordeal – their ship had been torpedoed.

Two or three days ago we picked up two Italian pilots from a plane that had been shot down during an action & I had a good time with them as I was the only one who could talk to them. I knew doggerel Argentine and they spoke doggerel Spanish & together with pencil & paper and much gesticulation we got on really well – if the Admiralty will pass what information (prohibited) they gave me I'll send it home to the journal (St John's) because it makes very interesting reading – so look out for it in about two months time. While at sea I've managed to celebrate Holy Communion daily & as far as possible try to remember King's *(Hospital)* & you all on Thursdays....

Love to you all

From

G Lawrence

LUCK or FATE

CHARLIE KNELL

LINESMAN, ROYAL CORPS OF SIGNALS

Charlie 1943 (author)

Charlie Frederick Hector Knell was born in 1916 at No1 Abbey Street Faversham, later demolished and now an access road to the Creek.

At the outbreak of war in 1939 he was married to Molly Cork and living at Teynham in Kent. He was 'excused boots', that is, excused call up for military service because he was in a reserved occupation. He was a carpenter by trade and at outbreak of war his company was employed by the government to build anti invasion gun emplacements and tank traps on the coast at Leysdown on the Isle of Sheppey. As a carpenter he would make the shuttering in wood for the concrete to be poured into. To make these various shapes in plywood needed skill and required a good knowledge of mathematics and geometry, this he had gained from an elderly man as a lad whilst working at a steel works at West Street in Faversham.

From time to time, they were attacked from the air by German planes that would strafe the beach where they were working. They dug a trench nearby and covered it over with a steel plate. They hung a piece of steel pipe up and at the first sound of aircraft approaching it was banged as a gong, to warn everyone to take cover in the trench.

The tank traps that Charlie helped to construct. Here being put to good use 80 years later by the local council to stop vehicles driving onto the seawall at Leysdown. Here they are shown upside down. (author)

His next job was at Jarman's Boat Yard at Conyer, building and repairing landing craft and boats for the Royal Navy. Then in 1941 he was working on constructing a minesweeper ship base at Queenborough and Sheerness dockyard. There he was involved in an industrial accident and quite badly injured. He was working sixty feet up on a scaffolding around a water tower when a heavy bucket used for hoisting cement up the building, instead of being lowered properly was just dropped from the top to the ground. As it plummeted down it hit a scaffold board which brought the other end up under Charlie's chin and broke his jaw in several places. He was taken to Sheerness Hospital but discharged they not having found the fractures. Although still in pain he returned to work the following day. On returning home from work a few days later he found his call up papers to join the army had arrived. The defence works were finished, and the threat of invasion had diminished. He was to join the Royal Corps of Signals as a linesman and report to the army camp at Catterick in Yorkshire.

Cap badge of the Royal Corps of Signals

He enjoyed the physical training and thirty-mile cross country runs, but found his jaw hurt so bad that one day he complained and said he couldn't go on a particular run that day. The instructor thought he was putting it on to get out of running and gave him extra guard duty. The pain got very bad and eventually he reported to the Medical officer, who realised that Charlie had a serious injury to his jaw that the previous hospital had failed to detect. He was sent down south to the hospital at Maidstone and after examination there was sent on to the Queen Victoria hospital at East Grinstead. This is where the now famous surgeon, Archibald McIndoe and his team were treating the burned air crew with pioneering plastic surgery and bone reconstruction work. He underwent two operations on his jaw there. Because these operations were experimental the procedures were recorded and photographed. One of the nurses working for McIndoe, nurse Mollie Lentaigne, was a gifted artist, so for future reference he employed her to sit in at all his pioneering operations and illustrate the procedures as they were carried out. At the same time, she also doodled other humorous drawings! Charlie was shown the photographs and drawings after his operations. These records were initially preserved at the hospital but have now been transferred to the East Grinstead museum.

Mollie Lentaigne, circa 1940

Mollie's drawings of the procedures during Charlie's operations.
(East Grinstead hospital)

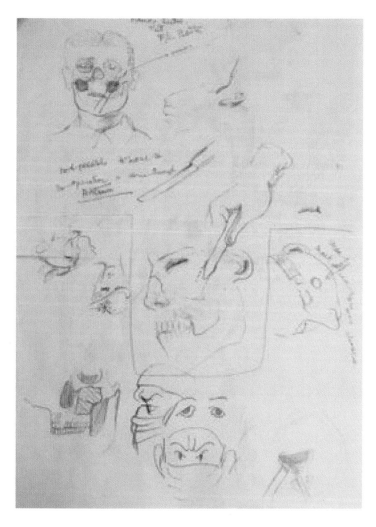

Charlie's operations recorded. On the left-hand side can be seen some of Mollie's 'doodles' (upside down), fashion of the forties and expressions on the faces of medical staff. The drawing top left is of Charlie and typical of his hairstyle a that time with a central parting.(East Grinstead Hospital)

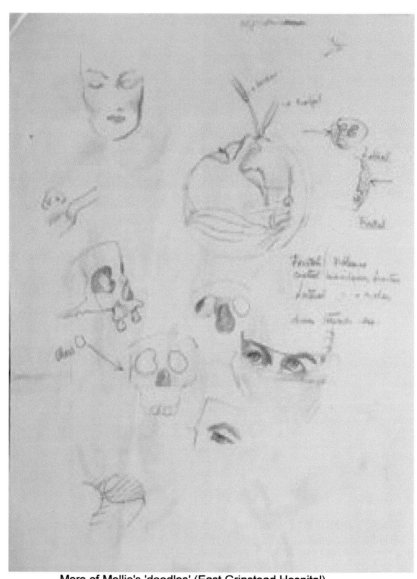

More of Mollie's 'doodles' (East Grinstead Hospital)

A Portrait of Archibald McIndoe and a self portrait by Mollie Lentaigne, 'doodled' during Charlie's operations. (East Grinstead Hospital)

Whilst Charlie was convalescing, he busied himself in the wards serving meals to and helping the badly burned air crew that McIndoe was experimenting on. They became known as members of the Guinea Pig Club. As soon as Charlie was reported as fit enough, he was called back to Catterick to continue his training, although he was then reclassified as B2 from A1 for fitness. He recalled how the officer in charge gave a talk to the new recruits and Charlie remembers him saying, "You are now gentlemen of the Royal Corps of Signals and as

such you will shave every day, even if you only have a piece of broken glass and a puddle". They were taught how to lay reels of telephone cable from the back of a moving lorry. As the lorry drove along the road they unwound and threw the cable over hedge rows and trees. They were taught how to erect an eighty-foot radio aerial in just three minutes using a cantilever method. They then connected this to a mobile telephone switchboard. After use it was quickly dismantled and moved so that the enemy could not get a fix on them.
He was also taught fundamental electronics.

Out in the field he could ring Molly, his wife in Kent by climbing a telegraph pole and connecting a phone to the wires. She didn't have a telephone at home, but he would have written to her and told her to be at the local village shop, who did have a phone, at a certain day and time.

By connecting to the wires Charlie could ring Molly in Kent (telegraph Ass.)

On completion of their course they were notified of their next posting. This was his next stroke of luck. He was posted to Taunton in Devon and was to be billeted in an old Malt House which had been commandeered by the army.

Most of the rest of his class were attached to regiments being sent to Singapore where, shortly after their arrival they were captured by the Japanese. They spent many years as POWs, many suffered, and many died there. See the story 'A Guest of Nippon'.

The next step to his survival came when, on arrival at the Malt House he found a new army issue carpenters tool set in the cellar. Shortly after arriving there a sergeant had reversed his lorry into something and badly damaged the tailgate. Charlie offered to repair it, it would save the sergeant getting into trouble. He removed all the metal work from the broken wood and rebuilt it, repainted it and no one would have known it had been damaged. The sergeant then asked him if he could make him a notice board. He agreed to make one, which would probably only take him a couple of hours...but he took three days! Because of shortages of materials and the manufacturers being engaged in war work there were no toys to be had in the shops. So Charlie used the time to make toys for his and his friends children. He made tanks using brass shell cases from .303 bullets, forts, castles, scooters and wooden Spitfires. Paper was difficult to come by so he set his plane deep and using a piece of wood eleven inches long and three quarters of an inch wide he made paper chains from dyed wood shavings. His activities came to the notice of the sergeant who instead of putting him on a charge, asked him to make his children some toys. It then became common knowledge and the officers heard of his activities...and ordered some for their children! It was an extremely cold winter so all the off cuts of wood were burnt on the pot bellow stove to keep warm.

Most of the men on the camp were drafted off to other postings but this was Charlie's next bit of luck, he was retained there to finish the toys! There was six inches of snow and many telegraph lines were brought down, which, fortunately for the local authority the Signal Corps were quickly able to repair.

As the saying goes, 'All good things must come to an end' and in the early part of 1944 and in preparation for D-Day a large exercise was planned in which Charlie would be taking part. This would be over several days and cover several counties. They would be laying telephone cable from a moving lorry for miles at a time. The exercise started in Dorset and would end in Lincolnshire where he would then be based.

Every now and again they had to erect the aerials and connect the mobile telephone exchange, then move on. In the early hours of the third day, they had reached Lincolnshire very tired having had little sleep. They were travelling on a long straight road when the driver of his lorry fell asleep at the wheel and missed a sharp bend. The lorry went over and down a twenty-foot embankment rolling over several times. Charlie came too to find he was trapped by his left arm. The window had been open at the time and as the lorry turned over Charlie's arm was thrown out the window, when the lorry came to rest the weight of the cab was on his arm. He could not get out on his own and he feared the lorry would catch fire because the grass was soaked in petrol. His luck was in again because a short time later a young midwife who had been out on a night call came across them. Charlie instructed her to get two big branches that were lying nearby, then by laying one alongside the cab and using the other as a lever and sitting on it she was able to raise the cab sufficiently for him to extricate himself. It was later found that his rifle, which had been propped up by his seat had gone through the canvas cover over the observation or machine gun hatch in the roof and when it was recovered, they found that the barrel was severely bent where it had been pushed into the soft ground and then hit a rock Now it may seem strange to say this, but the accident was yet another large piece of luck. Because after being hospitalised and his shattered arm had been operated on and set, he was on 'light duties' when the D-Day invasion took place.

Army lorry showing the observation or machine gun hatch over the passenger side in the roof. (Russ Sharp)

It probably saved his life because a visit to the D-Day Cemetery in France showed that many graves in the front row were men from his regiment. As it was, Charlie found himself billeted at Fort Widley. They had first suggested he could drive a lorry but then thought better of it because his broken bones were still green. "I know," said the sergeant, "You can go on the switchboard". He was given a green security card which gave him access to the top-secret communications centre in Fort Southwick at Portsmouth. The tunnels had been dug in 1942 by the Royal Engineers Tunnelling Section, they were

30m deep by 100m by 50m and more like an underground village.

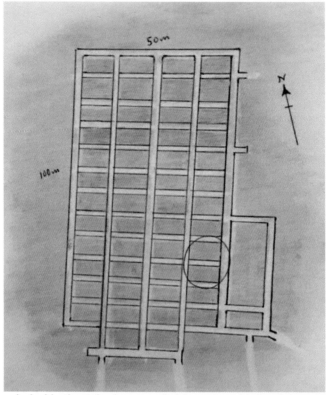

The area circled is the telephone switchboard and teleprinter area. At the top left and right were two entrance stairways and at the bottom several emergency exits. (author)

During D-Day there were up to 700 personnel in them and many more above ground supporting them. As well as a command centre and other specialist groups there were several switchboards and teleprinter rooms manned by members from the various services. Whilst on the switchboard he at one time found himself talking to Winston Churchill and putting him through to Eisenhower. As soon as he connected them, Churchill would say "Scramble old man",

One of the entrances to tunnels with over 100 steps to start a shift and walk back up afterwards! (Alan Murchie)

and no one could hear what they were talking about. The date of the invasion had been so secret that, even though there were rumours, and he was on the telephones, he was not aware of when it was to take place. Until one morning he emerged into daylight and saw that the hundreds of ships and landing craft of the invasion fleet that had been in Portsmouth, had all sailed.

When he became fit again, he was expecting to be shipped over to the battlefields on the continent. He had a bit of a personality clash with the new sergeant at the camp, he'd had an argument with him about having to stand more than others on night guard duties. He was given yet another night guard duty that day. However, lady luck or fate intervened yet again. That afternoon as he was marching across the parade ground, he bumped into the medical officer who was the surgeon who had treated him for his broken arm. He remembered Charlie and asked him how his arm was, Charlie told him that the arm wasn't too bad, but his damaged jaw was giving him trouble on cold days. The surgeon asked him how many children he had, Charlie told him four and another on the way. The officer then said, "The war is nearly over, with your injuries the best thing you can do is go home, work and provide for your family".

Having been to the office for the necessary paperwork and obtained a railway warrant, he was marching smartly towards the main gate when he heard a very loud voice shouting, "And where do you think you're going Knell?" Charlie waved the railway warrant in the air and said, "I'm obeying the last order sergeant... which was, **to go home**". He wore his army great coat home and, like many families in those hard times and before the days of the duvet, their army great coats were used on the children's beds as blankets.

The distortion to his broken arm was evident for the rest of his life.
Having arrived home he, along with others from Teynham village were presented with a silver-plated tankard by the villagers for their service to their country.

Charles Mapin & Webb Tankard

He immediately put his skills to good use and was working long hours repairing the shell and bombed damaged buildings in Deal and Dover. The workmen travelled by coach and sometimes slept there in the evening and then worked another shift through the night. Because of the lack of materials at the time he was cutting broken glass to fit smaller panes. Wooden doors that were warped were put into purgatory (*forced into the other direction*) to straighten and reuse them, splintered wood was cut down and reused such were the shortages after nearly five years of war. During his lunch breaks and using wood from broken furniture, he made picture frames and wooden animals on wheels for the children. Many of these he sold at Wigg's paper shop in Teynham and earned as much doing that as his weeks' wages. They sold for 7/6d, the shopkeeper kept 1/6d.

He went on to construct the shuttering on large projects like the Kingsferry Bridge over the river Swale to the Isle of Sheppey in Kent and the M2 motorway bridges, a very specialised job.

Two of Charlie's photo frames. The little girl is his great granddaughter, and the dog is Bob, his pet, in 1928.

The four children he had on leaving the army were to finally increase to eleven, five of whom would not be here if he had not survived... Luck or Fate?

SINKING OF HMS HARDY(II)

KEN DICKINSON
SIGNALMAN RN

The sleek classic destroyer HMS Hardy (II), the
replacement for the one lost at Narvik.

The following are short extracts from the memoirs of Ken
Dickinson, he was an ex WWII RN telegraphist and we met
aboard 'Cavalier'. Like many other men, he's recorded his
wartime experiences for the following generations of his family,
they are not published anywhere but he gave them to me, as
he said, 'So that if anything happens to him they will not get
lost'.

We take up the story as he rejoins HMS Hardy having
been temporarily loaned to another ship...The Norwegian
destroyer 'Stord'.

"A couple of days out from Gib. we were dispatched at
full speed to the Bay of Biscay to a position where HMS
Charybdis, a light cruiser had been sunk. After a few hours we

were recalled to join the fleet. We eventually tied to a buoy in Flotta, Scapa Flow without mishap or further action.

I was transferred to HMS Tyne the destroyer depot ship and then to 'Dunluce Castle', which was used as a billet for ratings waiting to join their ship. I again rejoined 'Hardy' on her return from a Russian convoy, glad that I had missed one.

When Flotta was crowded we often shared a buoy with HMS Maharatta, a powerful M class destroyer of D3 flotilla , she was built just pre-war. We crossed freely from ship to ship and made many friends in her crew when we joined in their tombola games. 'Maharatta' was a well-liked and respected veteran of Russian convoys. Her tragic end came in February 1944 a month after 'Hardy' was sunk in almost the same position. She was torpedoed twice. And just as HMS Impulsive, another friend with whom we shared buoys was trying to come alongside her, as later 'Venus' did with 'Hardy', 'Maharatta' rolled over and sank immediately. Only seventeen of a crew of over two hundred survived. Such is fate, or is it luck, or is it writ?

During this time, I can't remember anything specific except continuous sea time, a desperate lack of sleep, a cold and wetness until we started on 'Hardy's' last voyage. It was our job to lead the escorts of the Russian convoy JW56A. We sailed to Stornaway, capital of the Outer Hebrides Island of Lewis and anchored in the bay early one evening. The locals opened up the village hall, gave us refreshments and organised a dance. They gave us a much-appreciated good time. It seemed like ages since we had had contact with the outside world. I think the duty watch and motorboats crew had difficulty getting us all back onboard.

We steamed down to Lock Ewe to pick up the convoy: this was unusual as normally local escorts were used to save fuel for us on the longer voyage. Our usual routine was to take over off Iceland.

After we passed Cape Wrath we encountered the

80

granddaddy of all gales, terrific winds, huge seas and no visibility, our mess deck was its usual shambles of swirling water and our clothes and belongings swirling about in the morass. The convoy became scattered and the escorts couldn't round them up so all ships were ordered to regroup in Akureyi, northern Iceland. Most ships arrived in the next couple of days and were reassembled. We lay at anchor and awaited Admiralty instructions. The mountains around the fjord were high and I missed a signal from Murmansk W/T. Fortunately 'Venus' who had a much taller mast than us passed the signal by Aldis. I was called before the Captain but exonerated completely thanks to the Chief singing my praises and competence. Reception in Arctic conditions was always dodgy.

The waters in the fjord were calm when suddenly a great wind blew up and spray about eight feet high whipped across our decks; we had started dragging anchor and had to put to sea very quickly. All these delays made the convoy well behind schedule. (*The consequences of which will be seen later.*) Soon after leaving Iceland a German aircraft spotted the convoy and circled us, homing U boats into our calculated path. We then knew that a U boat pack would strike suddenly further along our route. We tried to ease out slowly to within gun range but he circled wider.

.........The weather continued bad but we struggled along with the convoy averaging about six knots. A couple of nights later the Commodores ship was torpedoed and sank along with two others. We arrived in the Kola inlet a few days later and as was usual immediately refuelled and restocked our depth charges, but as usual no food or stores.

Due to all our delays the following convoy, JW56B, was only two days behind us. This meant that the U boats that had gathered anticipating an earlier killing were still there, plus others that had joined them. The Admiralty intelligence estimated that fifteen U-Boats were in the path of the convoy.

This convoy was seeing a lot of action and were running out of depth charges; fortunately the bad weather prevented too many air attacks. It has to be realised the convoys could not alter course because of the pack ice.

Our Captain Robson, who was captain D, was instructed to take our flotilla out to help. And so we sailed with the weather improving. I was called to the wireless office to transmit a very long cipher message (about 250 five-figure groups) to escorts of JW56B. This signal gave their escorts our intended positions in protecting the convoy and the type of action we would take. The escort to JW56B was HMS Milne, D3. Cpt. Campbell. I keyed this message with my right hand; it was prefixed with priority code OU (most immediate) and transmitted on the Murmansk, Scapa and Iceland wavelength, a frequency kept by all warships. They could not break silence to reply or ask for repeats so I had to repeat my transmission which I did using my left hand! (Big show off) It was a strange feeling whacking out Morse code knowing that every U boat and German station in Norway were taking down my signal. 'Hardy' could transmit because she was a long way off from the convoy and would not give their position away.

Sometime later, I think it was night, but then it was always dark. I was in the W/T office when there was a terrific explosion from aft; the ship seemed to be lifted in the air and then dropped back down again. The engines stopped but the lights and the ventilation remained functioning. A few people uttered the word 'Christ' or words to that effect and went on working, signals continued to be received and we had to take them down and decode. After some time, maybe half an hour we could feel the deck tilting as the ship started to slip backwards. Our CPO was a great and considerate person who looked after our welfare. He put the main frequencies on loudspeaker, stayed in the office himself and told us to go on to the upper deck and inflate our lifebelts, which we always wore.

Outside the office the forecastle flat was bedlam but not panic as several parties were organising hoses and shoring material. One of our direction finding ratings that had been on watch aft looked at me and said; 'Got a tickler mate?' (*Self rolled cigarette*) I stayed on the upper deck looking aft where there was a fire and at that moment came another big explosion. The deck tilted to a greater angle and cold seawater crashed down over us. I was dressed in a jersey and pants as I had been on watch in the wireless office. Everything went very cold and people rushed past me and jumped into the sea. I climbed on the guardrail to follow, but when you are a non-swimmer an ice encrusted sea is not very inviting, so I stayed onboard. Very soon, about a minute, pitiful cries were coming from the sea. Our engineer officer launched the motorboat to pick up people from the freezing cold sea. The public address system was not working so the bosun's mate came round piping for all hands to muster on the forecastle. By this time the bows were higher out of the water and the ship sliding back further under the sea. Our captain joined us with a signalman with an Aldis lamp. The flotilla seemed to be doing a box search around us; some were directed to chase surrounding U boats. Suddenly HMS Virago nudged up to our bows and a few ratings had time to jump across before she slipped away. All the time pitiful cries for help were coming from the survivors in the water. I heard our captain make a signal to 'Venus', at that time a distant dark shadow; 'I have been struck aft come alongside to pick up survivors when prudent'. Considering our quarterdeck at that time was underwater I thought this to be a bit of classical RN officer's understatement! Very quickly 'Venus' came alongside in pitch darkness; I judged the gap and the movement of the two ships and jumped down on to the starboard side of 'Venus' forecastle. 'Hardy's' bows were by that time much higher than those of her sister ship as she continued to slip under. I was caught by four people and told to go below to keep the landing spots clear. 'Venus' had launched her whaler and picked up survivors from the water and in the forward mess deck the sickbay staff were attending to them. I saw two W/T colleagues lying on the deck, young Ken Smith, the York Minster organist and another youngster; we called 'Colonel' because his name was Lee. He was just nineteen, very likeable lad. We were told to rub hard on all their limbs to try to restore their circulation. However after a while the Doc came round, did a test and then pulled a cover over them. I then went up on the upper deck not dressed for the weather but not feeling anything, I saw 'Venus' torpedo tubes being turned out for firing. 'Hardy' was lying bows up about a mile away. A torpedo was launched over the side and it took ages to reach her. We could not see its track because of the dark, suddenly a great gush of flame shot up from 'Hardy' and she slid backwards slowly under the water. My mess deck was low in the bows of 'Hardy' and my locker was under the third scuttle. I remember the scuttle slipping under the water and thinking 'There goes my presents for Joan, Mum and Mary together with my 21st birthday gifts. Silly irrational thoughts but now I suppose that would be diagnosed as 'stress', a word then only used to describe the state of the ships ropes...

The following morning we were mustered on 'Venus' upper deck, where a roll call was taken, this to be checked against survivors picked up by other ships. A burial at sea was being organised for the afternoon. I walked round the upper deck where the bodies of my shipmates were being sewn into canvas bags, shipmates with whom I had been sharing food and conversation with only a few hours previously.

'Venus' was stopped and their bodies slipped from under the white ensign weighted down with a shell.

We were eventually taken to Polyarnoe in the Kola Inlet where trucks took us to Vaenga hospital dressed in spare kit donated by shipmates from 'Venus'. They were never compensated for their generosity. Nobby Hall, my old mate from Cleethorpes had given me a set of underwear, a charity knitted jersey and I had a tatty dirty old Duffel coat. These clothes, plus an issue leather fur hat, I wore till reaching Devonport some two weeks later.

I heard later that 'Impulsive' and 'Whitehall' sank a U boat shortly after 'Hardy' went down and 'Stord', the ship I had just left in Scapa, blew another U boat to the surface.

The official history states that the arrival of 'Hardy' and her flotilla turned a rout on the convoy into an attack and the U boats withdrew".

After survival leave, Ken was drafted to the frigate HMS Mounsey. On her he saw more action in the Atlantic, off Newfoundland and off Cherbourg and the invasion beaches of France, and then:

HMS Mounsey

"As November approached we were issued with arctic clothing and rumours of Russian convoys were doing the rounds, I was not excited!

We joined a convoy and were doing the miserable inner screen escort with the lovely big fleet destroyers dashing around on the outer screen. This time it was 'Onslow' D17, and the 'O' boats.

The convoy seemed fairly uneventful until I came off watch one night. I was not sure what time of the day it was as it was dark most of the time. Going aft to our mess the 'Doc' asked me if I would like a game of chess, which we sometimes played in the sickbay; this was just through a hatch from our mess deck. I declined his offer, put on a hat, coat, gloves, scarf etc. and went up on to the bridge. I had no business up there but it was interesting to see the officer of the watch conning the ship and I could chat to my pal Pete Shaw, a signalman.

I could hear the ping from the ASDIC repeater on the bridge. Suddenly without warning and no change in the ASDIC ping there was a loud explosion from aft and a great column of flame and smoke shot in the air. The ASDIC should have at least picked up the track of the torpedo but in Arctic conditions it was sometimes not very effective.

The captain was on the bridge immediately and I went aft and saw flames and smoke pouring from my mess.
I discovered later that the torpedo had entered my mess and killed all the occupants, the sickbay was also wrecked and the 'Doc' killed.

My life had been spared because of my experience on 'Hardy' causing me to spend as little time as possible over the propellers.

The bridge was constantly calling for the SBA to look after the wounded. I helped the burned and wounded to the captain's cabin, which was used as a temporary sickbay. I helped to apply dressings and ointments, which were in plentiful supply from the many first aid boxes. I made a point of telling mostly the dazed ones not to go over the side into the water unless 'abandon ship' was piped.

The ship was stopped and damage control parties were fighting hard to put out the fires. The wind was blowing from astern and fanning the flames so the skipper got another frigate to nudge us round, so that the flames blew aft over the stern. The other frigate took us in tow and we started the long journey to Polyarnoe.

The chefs still managed to provide us with a lovely meal of

'tiddy oggies' and chips. For pudding, we had the special tins of fruit salad (got earlier from Newfoundland), which we had been saving for Christmas dinner. A message was piped from the bridge that the torpedoing of a Devonport ship was not a serious enough event to spoil the ships favourite meal!

Our casualties were buried at sea the following morning from under the white ensign and with full prayers read by the captain.

Many of our stores had been destroyed and we ended up on ships biscuits and tinned brisket of beef.

And so I arrived in the Kola Inlet late in November. Whilst most of the rest of the crew went home I remained behind as a part of the Steaming Crew waiting for her repair to be completed…I had the unenviable prospect of sharing the delights of Polyarnoe, Vaenga and Murmansk for some time. Lucky me I had survived yet again…luck? Fate? Or was it writ"?

STALAG XXB (No26)
EAST PRUSSIA

PRIVATE 289700 ALAN FISHER

P.O.W. 6682

Alan Photographed with his mother at the time of his call up.

Alan George Fisher came from Sittingbourne in Kent. He was called up for military service in 1939 and joined the 5th Battalion, East Kent Regiment (known as The Buffs). In September 1939, along with the Royal West Kents, they were sent to Europe with the British Expeditionary Force in an attempt to deter the Germans from invading France. By May of 1940 the Germans had invaded and were forcing the BEF to retreat. On the 19th May 1940 they were ordered to retreat to Dunkirk to be evacuated back to Britain but were cut off. When they arrived at a town called Doullens they were ordered to halt and fight a rearguard delaying action. They were to hold the line for as long as possible in order that the majority of the troops could escape to the channel.

The Buffs dress cap badge

He was at Doullens at the same time as Hector Knell, also mentioned in this book. But Hector was one of those that were ordered to drive the troops away to escape. Alan was eventually captured along with many others and interned as a Prisoner of War (POW) by the Germans. It must have been an anxious time not knowing when or whether you would live to see home and family again. For the next five years he was to undergo some horrendous experiences and like a lot of men who had undergone them when they returned home, were rarely able to talk about it.

The captured troops were taken by lorry and rail towards Germany but then marched for hundreds of miles to prisoner of war camps. Alan's final destination was to be a POW camp near the village of Willenberg two miles south of Marienburg in East Prussia, and about twenty four miles south east of Danzig. (*In 1945 Danzig became the Polish Gdansk and Marienburg East Prussia was to become the Polish Malbork*). The camp was Stalag XXB No.26 (*Stalag short for Stammlarger*) and was run by the German Luftwaffe (*Airforce*). The camp consisted of wooden huts which were in poor condition, they having been used as a POW camp in the WW1 nearly forty years earlier.

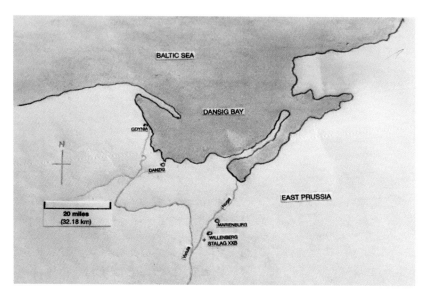

Willenberg and Marienburg, 24 miles south east of Danzig.

He was given the POW Number 6682 and they were then photographed. They were issued with nice clean uniforms for the photograph, which were afterwards taken off them. These photographs were then sent back to Britain via the Red Cross to show that the prisoners were being well treated and that the camp complied with the Geneva Convention. They had various other photographs taken from time to time to show that they were enjoying their captivity. They were allowed to send them home after they had passed the camp censor, who's stamp appears on the reverse of all of them.

As the photos were taken shortly after their capture, they still looked healthy. However, they were to endure five years of privation, many did not see the end of those five years. Occasionally they managed to eat well when they were attached to outside working parties, most of the time they survived on turnips or potatoes. It is known that he did his bit to be a thorn in the side of his captors.

POW camp photograph, Poland 1940,
Alan is fourth from the left middle row. (family)

On one occasion he and another POW had been on a working party and were taking a hand cart full of some good fresh vegetables from a farm to the German officers' mess.

A camp boxing tournament. Photo sent home by Alan (family)

Reverse of the above with Official Stamp. (Gepruft = Checked)

Just as they passed the main gate to the camp the main gate was opened for a vehicle to enter. Before he could be stopped Alan ran through the gate into the compound and tipped the vegetables off the hand cart onto the ground, where they were quickly snatch up by the hungry prisoners. For this he was given the standard punishment, which was the Strafe or Punishment Company. This consisted of three weeks in the 'Bunker' or isolation cell.

Putting on a stage play in camp.

Reverse of the above photo showing the official Stalag 'Checked' Stamp.
Alan's mother had remarried hence the different surname.

This cell was small with no windows just a small peep hole in the door. The toilet was a tin can, the bed and pillow was a one piece wooden bench with a single threadbare blanket, and this when temperatures could drop at night to -20c or even lower in the winter. The only food received when on punishment was a thin soup every two or three days and a piece of black bread which was fifty percent sawdust. There was no cutlery, so Alan had made a spoon out of a piece of wood. After his release from the cell, he was given three or four weeks of emptying the camp latrines, these as you can imagine had an unimaginable stench and there was always the chance of catching disease.

He was probably treated lightly by the Commandant, who had a certain amount of respect for him because of an incident that occurred earlier whilst he was out on a working party on a farm. A 13yr old girl fell into the freezing river Nogat, which ran near the camp, and none of the guards made a move to help her. Alan jumped in and pulled her out and gave her artificial respiration, unfortunately to no avail as she later died of hypothermia. However, the Commandant heard of the incident and of Alan's courageous efforts and commended him for his efforts. Information of what was going on in the war

93

filtered into the camp, it was known that there was a clandestine radio in one of the huts, however they never knew whether what they heard was genuine information, rumour or propaganda. In 1945 as the Russians fought their way towards the camp, the German guards were for a short while confused and unsure what was to happen to the prisoners. The prisoners awoke one morning to find there were no guards on the gate. The British officers advised their men to stay put until the Russians arrived. Most of the men did and some made off towards the Russian lines. Alan and his friend Fred Spells decided to commandeer (*steal*) a German Officers Mercedes Staff car and drove off towards Danzig. They were hoping to find a ship there to board. Shortly after they had left the camp the German troops were ordered by Hitler to march the prisoners back towards Germany to be used as hostages. Luck or Fate had intervened for Alan and Fred. They probably didn't know it at the time, but they had left the camp when there was a short window of a few hours when it was not guarded. Those that went for the Russian lines were not looked after very well and it took nearly a year to get home, in the meantime they had been half starved. The remainder of the over 7,000 prisoners were forced to march hundreds of miles, starving and in freezing conditions in what became known as the so-called notorious Death March. Those that could not keep up were shot out of hand. It was estimated that almost a third of them died before reaching Germany and eventually the allied lines.

The Russians left a terrible legacy in the area, German women were raped and murdered, and all the German children shot. It was thought in revenge for the terrible atrocities that the Germans had inflicted on Russian families. Many years later mass graves were discovered nearby in Danzig.

For Alan and Fred, it must have been a nightmare experience driving through the chaotic bombed roads and villages. Bearing in mind that the land was in Prussia and still a part of Germany, so the roads were crowded with German civilians as well as some troops, fleeing the impending Russian onslaught. They were trying to get to the evacuation ships in the port of Danzig in order to get back to Germany by ship. The Germans had organised the evacuation under the code name Operation Hannibal. However, it was implemented too late and descended into chaos.

Before arriving at the port Alan and Fred decided it safer to abandon the car and walk the last couple of miles, rather than get caught with a German Officers Staff car! there were still many German troops making for the port. They wrecked it and pushed it off the road over a bank so that it could not be used again by the Germans. They walked through the chaos and blended in with other fleeing civilians. They found their way to the port where, to their relief there were several Allied ships in the harbour.

There was also a merchant ship that had been sent in by the Swedish Red Cross and explaining who they were they were allowed to board. In the Bay it was still a very confused and dangerous situation.

German civilians and troops fleeing the Russian advance into East Prussia.
(Bundesarchiv, Bild 146-1976-072-09)

The bombed Marienburg Castle was on the opposite bank of the Nogat to
XXB camp, a part of which was used as an extension to the camp. (Simon
Sheppard drypool.com)

Bombed buildings at Marienburg. (National Museum of US Air Force)

Many hundreds of German troops and civilians died when the rescuing ships were torpedoed in Danzig Bay by a Russian submarine. The German Red Cross ship, the 'Wilhelm Gustloff', with some 10,000 German nationals onboard was torpedoed leaving Danzig Bay, with an estimated 9000 women, children and troops drowned. (*One of the worst recorded maritime losses of life*) They had tried taking some POWs with them onboard as hostages, but a Royal Navy destroyer arrived and stopped them. The Red Cross ship Alan and Fred boarded was finally able to sail and they were to see home for the first time in five years. It's difficult to imagine how they must have felt, it must have been so emotional. They had survived five years of captivity and come through some very dangerous situations. Luck or Fate?

Alan was to go on to have a lovely family. Fred Spells was to remain a lifelong friend, he was god parent to Alan's daughter who was named after Fred's wife Madeline.

Alan later became a driving instructor and very often recalled that he had smashed up a lovely expensive Mercedes car and then had to struggled to buy a cheap car for his work at home.

It's unlikely that Alan and Hector Knell ever met up during the chaos that was war time Doullens, but as a coincidence many years later, Alan's daughter Madeline went on to marry Hector's nephew Roger Knell.

A GUEST OF NIPPON

WILLIAM E, GUEST

SIGNALMAN 2341310
ROYAL CORPS OF SIGNALS

In June 1942 during WWII the Japanese decided to build the Burma – Siam railway in order to be able to transport troops and supplies to Burma and Malaya. Before the war the Americans had turned down the offer to build a railway here because of the loss of life it would entail in the fetid jungle. Of course it didn't matter to the Japs who were using thousands of POWs as labourers, it didn't matter to them how many died! This railway crossed several rivers and ravines which had to be bridged, the most well known being the bridge over the river Kwai. William Guest, captured at the fall of Singapore in 1941, was, amongst others sent to work on this railway. Very few survived the horrendous conditions and the harsh treatment meted out by the Jap Guards. It was estimated that some 13,000 allied troops and 80 – 100,000 civilians died in its building. Against all the odds Bill not only survived but kept a diary on any scraps of paper he could get hold of.

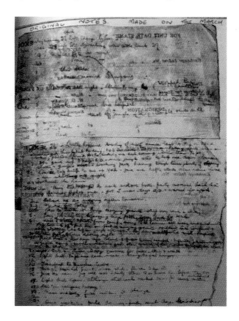

Bill kept a diary on any scrap paper he could find

This is Bill's story.

Bill came from Redbrook Road, Gawber, Barnsley, Yorkshire. He joined the Royal Corps of Signals in November 1940. After six months training at Catterick Army camp he qualified as a wireless operator and was sent on to Bakewell in Derbyshire. This camp was specifically set up to kit out and prepare soldiers for an over seas posting. He received his tropical kit and on the 3rd January 1941 found himself with his regiment onboard the 25,000 liner S.S. Empress of Japan (ironically as it turned out).

At this stage they had no idea of their final destination. They stopped at Freetown, South Africa, then Mombasa, Cape Town and Bombay. After nine weeks at sea they arrived at their final destination...Singapore. The food on the ship had been excellent as was their reception at all the ports they called at, especially Cape Town. There he said he met a very nice young lady, Ruth Kadish, she was later to write to his mother enquiring after Bill when she heard of the fall of Singapore.

At Singapore they were transported to a tented encampment in Ulu Pandau, an outer suburb of Singapore. For him Singapore had conjured up visions of sandy beaches, swaying palms and scantily clad young girls The reality was completely different with smelly monsoon drains with dead dogs and the like in them.

After a short stay in Singapore they were transported to Sungie Patani, a small native village about 26 miles north of Panang in North West Malaya. It was a very large rubber plantation not far from the Thai border.

When the Japanese declared war there were no Royal Navy ships in these waters and the RAF only had 200 ancient planes. In late November condensation trails of enemy planes started to appear daily. The Japs landed and without air support after a few days fierce fighting the line broke and the retreat started. A few stands were made in the hope that help would come soon but enemy aircraft were bombing and machine gunning us without opposition. In the first two weeks we lost twelve out of twenty six signals offices and the 9th and 11th divisions had suffered so many casualties that they had to combine to make one division, the 9\11[th].

We retreated onto Singapore Island but were soon surrounded. They captured the water supply making it intolerable. The hospitals were filled to over flowing owing to civilian bombing casualties. It was thought that up to 20,000 civilians had been killed on that last day.. Then the hospitals were over run by the enemy who proceeded to bayonet the patients in their beds. They took the medical orderlies out side and machine gunned them all, including a doctor who had been operating on a patient.

Last minute attempts were made to evacuate women and children from the island but most of the ships that did get away were torpedoed and sunk with great loss of life.

When the surrender came I was working in GHQ on the switchboard. We remained in the office all night and in the morning discovered that the locals had looted our stores, I therefore started life as a POW with just the clothes I stood up in plus a haversack with a few bits in.

The first sight of our guards were the Japanese front line troops. What a reg tag lot they appeared to us, accustomed as we were to the British army B- S-. Short, thick set, unwashed and unshaven, dressed in rags with ignorance written all over their evil looking yellow faces.

We did not expect to live but as we found out later they must have had orders to save us as a labour force. They took watches, gold rings and anything of value from us and ordered us to sit and await further orders. We were kept under guard.

The next day we had to march the 26 miles to Changi prison. Although it was not particularly nice there but I would later wish I were back there! There was very little seen of the Japs there for a while and we organised our own rationing of the supplies we had. Breakfast was 3 hard tack biscuits and a teaspoon of bacon. Tiffin (lunch) was 2 biscuits and jam, a cup of tea and a little stew. Cigarettes ran out and was a foretaste of what was to come. The Japs then took over feeding us with plain boiled rice flavoured with anything to be got hold of. Or burnt to give it a different flavour!

We were employed in Singapore burying the thousands of dead civilians and Japs who died in their suicide charges. We were ordered to salute or bow to our captors, failure to do so earned you a beating. Marching through the gate one day we were accused of being slovenly and disrespectful, the officer was severely beaten and the troops made to slap each other round the face, if not hard enough the guard would do it again.

The lack of food started to tell on the health of the men. The first of my friends to die was Nobby Clark from Sheffield.

In September we were all asked to sign a non escape form.

We all refused and as a result we were all herded on to Selarang Square, the peace time parade ground. An estimated 19,000 men, 2,000 became hospital cases. The Japs then threatened to take the patients from the hospital onto the square and at that the officer commanding ordered them to sign. Four men still refused and were dragged out and shot several times by ignorant and inexperienced troops. (After the war the Jap general responsible was hanged for war crimes).

Diphtheria and other diseases were rife and about six men a day were dying from them. I spent several weeks in hospital with Dip, and Dip paralysis. I considered myself lucky that the rest of my unit in the meantime had been sent to Japan to work in the coal mines. However there was a big move afoot and an interpreter informed us that a big camp had been built 'up country' under Red Cross supervision and it was their intention to send everyone who could walk to this 'paradise'... and we believed them! So much so that we took musical instruments and all sorts of kit. At Singapore station we boarded a box car with sliding doors. After a weary night we arrived in Kuala Lumpur where we were allowed off for an hour to eat our first meal of rice and vegetable water since leaving Changi. The next stop was at Prai on the 29th. There was a lack of water and we suffered in the heat of the iron box car. We took it in turns to lay on what space there was on the floor. There were no toilet facilities.

After five days with very little water we came to Banpong (Bahnpong). This was a transit camp for working parties going up to the rail head. Anything past here was thick fever ridden jungle with very few tracks. The forced march to get to the rail head was 200 miles, many failed to live to see the end of it. The guards were changed daily. All of the equipment we had brought from Changi was dumped at Banpong. My feet were blistered. During one dark night when we stopped I managed to contact a native, I bartered everything I had, including what I stood up in for a few biscuits and bananas, without which I would not have made it.

Bahnpong transit station

It got so bad that without the help of two men, Asprey from London and Perry (who later died) I would not have made it. We took it in turns to prop each other up whilst one slept in the middle whilst marching... left, right, left, right, everything became hazy. I bound my feet up like a mummy, the boots had long gone. We stopped at an encampment, the conditions were indescribable with swarms of flies in the stinking heat. The next day was much the same except there were swarms of mosquitoes which descended on us en masse and followed us for miles. As if things couldn't get any worse we were informed that rough country lay ahead and we were to undergo a medical examination. Those unfit would be left behind...to what? Suspecting what would happen to them, all of those who could struggle to walk did so. We left several behind to their fate.

That night we passed a small Kampong (huts/village) little knowing that it would be the last civilisation that many would ever see and those that survived would never forget.

The track became a mere treacherous dusty path. The dust that was kicked up made our thirst worse.

The events of the next two weeks are hazy. Night after night we marched on, resting during the heat of the day. After each stop our numbers decreased! Cholera broke out as a result of some men, being so thirsty drank water from the rivers. The water was normally boiled but there was never enough of it.

By the 11th the distance covered nightly decreased because of the terrain and sheer exhaustion.

The rest camp myth was exploded as we passed through a camp where prisoners were making railway sleepers from logs. Each day fresh guards were changed in order to drive us on. The reason for their haste became obvious when on the 20th and within minutes the track was under several inches of thick mud. My footwear had long given up and I resorted to bare feet. The torrential rain was incessant. During the stops I was so tired that I just lay down in the mud to sleep.

On Saturday 22nd April after marching 200 miles we arrived at our new 'home'- Sunkrai or No2 work camp. The camp was pretty rudimentary, Iron cooking pots had been sunken in the ground which were covered by a bamboo frame work covered in banana leaves. Behind this primitive cook house was a hill which became known as 'Cholera Hill', which is where men who had cholera were sent to die. A bit further on were some half built huts with no roofs...this was our 'Rest Camp'. On arrival there we had a roll call, out of the 100 in my section only 51 had survived! The total camp strength was roughly 1,500.

We immediately set too to make a secure hut for the sick, because it was still raining heavily. Until our numbers slowly decreased there was very little room to sleep, we were top to toe.

We were immediately put to work levelling the ground.

Reveille, or Bango, was at 0530hrs, breakfast was a handful of plain rice, the midday meal was the same as was the evening meal. Living as we were under terrible conditions two of the Manchester's died the first day. The second day seven died, by the end of the week twenty had died. On the 29th a further seven went to Cholera Hill. Conditions were appalling and sanitation primitive. Dysentery then broke out and spread through the camp like wild fire, by the end of May only 50 men were able to work. The Japs realised that something had to be done when some of their men went down with it. We were given two days rest, out of expediency, not out of humanity.

All suspect cases were placed in a hut away from others. There was no serum or medicines so an injection of saline made from ordinary salt was given. The men died still crying out for water.

We were then working in the quarries and each morning we passed the bodies of those who had died during the night. You felt lucky that you were alive. You got so used to it that you could no longer sympathise for your comrades. It was raw nature, survival of the fittest. I awoke one morning to find both the men either side of me had died during the night.

The Monsoon continued and the ground got so bad that nothing could move. Food was rationed to two small portions of rice a day. We supplemented that with a stew like substance made from bamboo and banana shoots and ginger root and anything else we thought edible.

Soon the only food to come into the camp was rice brought by a working party floundering through ten miles of muddy track.

By this time we ceased to resemble human beings.

The Japs contemptuously called us White Coolies. What clothes we had were rags and most men just wore a make do 'G' string. No boots, no soap, just lousy scarecrows. The bridge over the river Kwai was in danger of being washed away by the torrent caused by the monsoon and we were to replace it. Half a mile from the camp was the quarry. The guards sat on an outcrop watching us as hour after hour we broke up rocks that had been blasted out of the rock face. Other men bored holes for the next days blasting. The only relief we got was at midday when the guard shouted "Yasumi" and we could sit and eat a handful of cold dry rice.

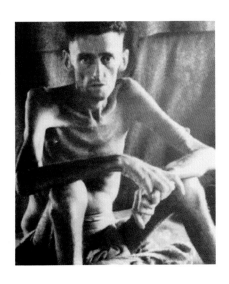

Starved and wasted we ceased to resemble human beings.(Forces.net)

Our muscles ached under the weight of the hammer, I learned to hold the hammer over my shoulder when the guard wasn't looking and let it fall when he looked my way. The danger was that if he caught you slacking he was only too ready to use his 'persuader' stick across your bare back. If splinters of rock cut you they were likely to turn to dangerous tropical ulcers. I was the only one left capable of work out of the 25 men I started work with in the quarry.

I realised that your position in the parade in the morning usually decided which job you would get, so I took up position at the end of the queue. One morning I ended up on a team cutting trees down, usually teak. These were for the construction of the new railway bridge spanning the river. It was back breaking work and we were beaten regularly with bamboo poles or ropes ends if we didn't move fast enough. In our weakened condition we dropped a log which crashed down a ravine. For this we were made to kneel on sharp flints for two hours and then we were approached by the 'Bull' as we called him, with his sword drawn, I said to my mate, "We've had it chum". He gave us all a blow over the head with the flat of the blade and then we had to endure a lecture on disobedience and its consequences and that we were being shown merciful forgiveness which will not be repeated, Woe betide anyone who does not work hard for the Emperor.

The next job was pile driving the trees into the river bed. A heavy iron weight hanging on ropes over a scaffold was lifted by thirty men to a monotonous chant of "Eni, Seni, Sio" – thump, (One, two, three- thump). It was dangerous work, if the weight rose unevenly the tower overturned and took the men with it. I saw one man crushed and thrown into the valley below. We were driven to speed up the work and the rumour was that the railhead was getting nearer to our camp.

The monsoon ended, but with the increased hot humid weather the midges returned. There were the normal body lice but also what were called Bamboo Lice, the result being that we were covered in running sores. Dysentery broke out again with the millions of flies from the trench latrines and with the men in weakened starving condition this often proved fatal. Some with ruptured stomachs and no medicines had to eat powdered charcoal. Huge ulcers developed and being literally alive grew bigger by the day and ate the flesh until bone showed. We were lucky to have a Colonel MO amongst the prisoners and he carried out about 26 amputations using a boiled sterilised saw borrowed from a working party, it was given back to them afterwards.

Out of the original 1,500 men there were now only 110 left! The Japs then brought up another group of Australian prisoners. I worked with the Aussies for a while until I went down with a bad spell of Jungle Fever and ended up in hospital on and off until September. The line was finally laid and the Japs decided to evacuate us.

We were loaded onto a train and taken back...I was lucky I had survived... We were in open trucks so crowded that we could not sit down properly, it was freezing cold at night but sweltering by day with no shade from the sun. I suffered my eleventh bout of jungle fever and was in a semi coma most of the trip. The five days it took could have been no hardship after the trials of the last few months, and anyway we were on our way back to Changi which seemed to us almost like going back home!

On arrival at Changi we were helped down from the transport by the other prisoners who were anxiously enquiring after friends. What a sight we must have presented, weak from starvation and disease, unwashed with long hair and beards crawling with lice. The prisoner medical officer put us into quarantine away from the other prisoners until we had been deloused and our rags had been burnt. We were issued with new shorts that someone had made from tent canvas. My weight was checked and found to be 7 stone 2 lbs and I was treated for dysentery.

Once recovered I was put to work with thousands of Indians and Chinese coolies extending the runway of the Changi airfield, our backs were white with salt in the sun.

One memorable day there came a sound we had almost forgotten- the sound of anti aircraft guns down by the harbour. Then we stared unbelieving as vapour trails appeared very high as to be almost invisible. They were our planes. Camp moral was lifted when we saw bombs and incendiaries showering down onto the warehouses.

We were all moved into what used to be a prison and were packed in so tight it was difficult to find space to lie down. The officers were separated for the first time. Food became even scarcer, with just plain rice flavoured with any green leaves they could get hold of. The lack of vitamins meant that all the men suffered from Beri-beri. Long after I got got home I could stick a pin in my limbs and draw blood but felt nothing.

It still took six agonising months before the British troops arrived, six months which many men did not get to see. It was an anxious time with the guards becoming more violent if we showed signs of enthusiasm when we saw our planes. We heard the rumour that the war in Europe had ended. When a rumour went round about the atom bomb being dropped there was a distinct change in the guards attitudes and they steered clear of us. We were allowed a small amount of sugar and other luxuries from Red Cross parcels previously denied us.

I'll never forget the night that we got the news of the dropping of the second atom bomb and the Japanese surrender. Happiness, bewilderment, some staring into space, some going crazy laughing and shouting. The officers however quietened everyone down, warning that the guards may take it out on us.

The next day the Japs sent in tons of supplies of European food into the gaol, tinned stewed meat and vegetables. We were warned not to eat too much as our stomachs could not take it. One Aussie died having eaten half a 7lb tin of bully beef!

A week later planes dropped army officers to take over command of the area, they kicked the Japs out of their offices, who were then running errands, and bowing and scraping. The Japs were ordered to salute all their ex prisoners and it was a treat to see. It was another three weeks, which felt like months, before the West Yorkshire Regiment arrived.

A loud speaker was installed to keep us in touch with what was happening and a cinema was erected down by the hospital. As many men who were able sat on the grass gazing in rapture at the colourful scenes of 'The Princess and the Pirate'.

We crowded round a war correspondent for news from home and he waved us back saying "Keep back a bit, you fellows really do smell"!

Before Mountbatten visited, the lawn at Raffles Square had been picked blade by blade by Jap prisoners. They had been taken into Singapore and disarmed. The officers and the worst of the criminal guards were placed in Outram Gaol to await trial.

What a pity we are so called humane people. Our troops protected the Japs from the Chinese people who wanted to take revenge. Some of us would like to have seen the Chinese let loose, they had suffered so much under the Jap occupation.

At last the day came for us to embark for home. We were driven down to the docks on lorries and it was a grand feeling to look down on the little yellow 'baskets' for the last time as they were being exercised under armed guard.

You can understand how we felt as the ship, the SS Tegleberg, sailed through the Malacca Straights in a calm blue sea and the islands slowly sank over the horizon. The realisation came to us that it was really all over.

SS Tegleberg. She and her two sister ships, the Ruys and Boissevain, were on charter from the Dutch government to transport returning POWs to the UK and Australia from Singapore and Batavia (Indonesia). (SS Maritime)

From hell hole to luxury. The lounge of the Tegleberg.(SS Maritime)

Onboard ship, the Red Cross gave us regular issues of cigarettes, chocolate, biscuits, lemonade and bottle of beer a day. As we entered Colombo harbour it was crowded with warships and invasion craft and the air was filled with the screeching of sirens and cheering men.

On the way home many of the men put on an extra two stone.

Our arrival in Liverpool would be forever remembered. We looked down into a sea of happy smiling faces. Tears rolled down cheeks. Those with relatives living nearby rushed to meet them while a few silent ones scanned each face as they descended the gangway. There was a buffet for us while we waited for transport to Huyton Transit Camp a few miles away.

We underwent rigorous medical checks and had x-rays to check for TB.

We were kitted out and we said our goodbyes to the men who had suffered together.

On the train home it felt strange to be sitting with civilians for the first time since 1941. I felt so self conscious in my new battle dress and yellow skin.

As the train pulled into Barnsley station I searched through the window to see who had come to meet me, but didn't recognise anyone.   I felt a nervous tension from the journey and the feeling of absolute freedom it had created. I had to think of the problem of carrying my two heavy kit bags with my depleted strength. As I lifted one to my shoulder a voice said "I'll take one Bill". I looked in amazement at a stranger who was four inches taller than me. He said "Don't you know me ?", I then realised it was my younger brother who when I saw him last was a boy in short trousers. I thought the events of the last three and a half years had hardened me to anything but I must confess this unexpected transformation unnerved me. I realised what a changed world lay ahead. Children had grown up. Old people gone.

For all those who had been prisoners, without news or papers to read time had stood still.

Now the future lay ahead in a changed world and the hope which had proved the mainstay of those who had survived the years of hardship was at last justified....Home at last.

Luck or fate? Bill had survived.

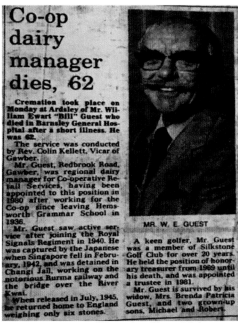

Co-op dairy manager dies, 62

Cremation took place on Monday at Ardsley of Mr. William Ewart "Bill" Guest who died in Barnsley General Hospital after a short illness. He was 62.

The service was conducted by Rev. Colin Kellett, Vicar of Gawber.

Mr. Guest, Redbrook Road, Gawber, was regional dairy manager for Co-operative Retail Services, having been appointed to this position in 1980 after working for the Co-op since leaving Hemsworth Grammar School in 1936.

Mr. Guest saw active service after joining the Royal Signals Regiment in 1940. He was captured by the Japanese when Singapore fell in February, 1942, and was detained in Changi Jail, working on the notorious Burma railway and the bridge over the River Kwai.

When released in July, 1945, he returned home to England weighing only six stones.

MR. W. E. GUEST

A keen golfer, Mr. Guest was a member of Silkstone Golf Club for over 20 years. He held the position of honorary treasurer from 1969 until his death, and was appointed a trustee in 1981.

Mr. Guest is survived by his widow, Mrs. Brenda Patricia Guest, and two grown-up sons, Michael and Robert.

(Barnsley Chronicle)

Kamchanaburi cemetery with over six thousand re-interred allied POW dead. One of three such cemeteries. (CWWGC)

BLOWN UP TWICE

WALTER FREDERICK CORK

LABOUR CORP, PRIVATE 1063
and
THE BUFFS, LANCE CORPORAL 446709

WWI

Walter Frederick Cork

Walter Frederick Cork was born at Bilsington in Kent, in 1885. His mother Elizabeth was one of the first trained midwives, his father George was a farm labourer. They tended to move about the county wherever their work took them. In his early twenties the family moved to Teynham in Kent and Walter along with many of his friends joined the East Kent Regiment, the 'Buffs' Territorial Army Unit and attended regular meetings at Faversham.

He met his future wife Bessie Beaney at the laundry owned by her stepmother, Frances Cullen, in Greenstreet. They married in 1911 at Bessie's village of Bobbing near Sittingbourne.

War clouds gathered and World War one broke out in 1914. This was when the Territorial army became a proper army instead of a 'club' for the lads. He was in the 2/4th Battalion and obtained the rank of Lance Corporal. At the outbreak of war, the 2/4th Battalion was immediately sent to India to relieve the regular army out there in order that they could return to Britain and the front line.

Non-Commissioned officers of the 2nd/4th Buffs Regiment. Walter is second from the left in the front row. The man on his right was Ben Hall, his friend who had been best man at his wedding. Many years later and unbeknown to them at the time both men's descendents were to meet and marry. Second from the right middle row is John Holland. (author)

However only single men went to India or France at the beginning of the war, so Walter and some of his friends, as married men, remained and were attached to the 7th Battalion.

The 7th Battalion was newly formed at Ashford under Lt Col Skey and they were attached to the 55th Brigade, IV army.

Initially they were guarding the coast and installations in Kent. As the war hotted up in 1915 he was sent for further training in Sunninghill and Ascot and then to Rochester and Sevenoaks.

In 1916 with casualties mounting in France, married men initially then married men with children were being sent to the battlefields. The time came for the 7th to be shipped to France, they were attached to the 55th Brigade in the 4th Army and were shipped over the channel on the British Rail train ferries. They didn't stay with the 55th Brigade for very long but were later moved around to counter German pressures on the line.

On arrival in France he was transferred to the Labour Corps to lay a small gauge railway track which would take ammunition up to the front. Later when they sent married men with children to the front he found himself with the Buffs in the trenches holding the line at Carnoy and Montauban. In that action 5 officers and 48 men were killed and 144 injured, among the dead was Capt. Neame VC from Faversham.

Walter had survived that battle. But then he was in a trench which, unbeknown to them had been undermined by the enemy with several tons of explosives. There was a huge explosion one day and only one survivor was found out of the 40 plus men in that section. Walter was found sometime later in a tree and still alive! That made two survivors. luck? Walter was transported back to a field hospital in the rear and then to Britain on a hospital train to convalesce. Can you imagine what it must have been like, having gone through all that to be told you are being ordered back to France and back in the trenches!

He was involved in battles all over France, among them Ypre, Bapaume - 26 killed, Amiens, Menier - 56 killed, Arras, Hazebroucke Rouquenet Wood with only 550 men left of the Battalion. For the next two and a half years there were numerous other battles of which he was lucky to survive.

Several of his friends had fallen alongside him.   Private
G/15821 McDonald Dixon, also from Teynham sent a post card
to his young daughter in England. He was killed at Cherisy on
the 3rd May 1917... his daughter received the card two days
later.

The post card McDonald sent his daughter.

Another friend, Nigel Wilcockson, wrote of his experience in

France and sent a letter to McDonald's family, a short extract follows below.

Then having been withdrawn from the line for rest, retraining and regrouping, they were in tents when one night there was an air raid by enemy aircraft, an unusual occurrence in those early days of flying. A bomb landed near Walter and he was injured again. There were several killed and 64 injured.

could one say that he was popular. In command was our former Platoon Officer Lieut [1] - his name I cannot remember just at the minute, who was very popular, took command of us when we went over. I was with him just before I believe he was killed. I remember we were then detailed for different duties and Dixon was appointed runner to Lieut - whose name I forget, but who commanded B Company when they went over that day or if not runner to him he was runner to our Sergeant Lockyer [2] who was afterwards taken prisoner. On the third day of our stay here, at dusk, we moved up to the front line. After we had gone a little distance we halted and I remember having a long talk here with Dixon and remember the conversation clearly.

We got into the line that night without mishap and the whole of the next day was very quiet but for an occasional shell and a couple of snipers who made us keep our heads down.

We had no chance of sleep that night [3] and the next morning at 3 o'clock under the direction of Lieut Wright we filed out through a gap in the parapet made by a shell and lay out on the ground a few yards apart from each other, awaiting the creeping barrage to start, even now the snipers still persisted. We did not have long to wait for the barrage which was a very good one [4] and we were soon following up in its wake.

Francis Herbert 2/Lt.

Extract from a letter to McDonald's family.

This time he was not sent home but to the rear to one of the field hospitals. (Incidentally those wooden hospital huts after the war were taken back to England and re-erected in many villages to become 'village halls'. Many of Walter's children would celebrate their marriages in the one at Teynham.

Having convalesced there, he was sent back into the line...

again.

When the war was over, he did not get back home straight away but his regiment were to stay in France as it was thought Germany may try to start the war again.

In January 1919 they were finally 'moved to Montigny to be readied for their demob. However, it took another six months for them to move to Dunkirk and finally sent home. The regiment had suffered 4864 killed. Walter and his friends Ben Hall and John Holland had survived. They arrived home to find very little work and Walter found it difficult to feed his large family. The farmer Mr Dixon, McDonald's father would occasionally give him food parcels.

During their time in France another of his friends, Sergeant John Holland, found that his wife and two children had been evicted from their home. Walter's wife Bessie took them in and cared for them. The two up two down house was crowded with her four children as well, times were hard.

Walter, passed away in 1971 but in 2008 his picture and details were published in a local paper. As a result Bernard, Walters son, received a call from Jack Holland, John Holland's son. He said he'd been trying to find Bernards family for years.

He said how he owed his life to Bessie and related how in 1916 as a child of a few months old. he contracted bronchial pneumonia and quickly became very ill. Bessie knowing time was vital rushed to the village doctor, Dr Selby, and persuaded him to visit the house, even though, there being no National Health Service, they could ill afford it. (they sometimes paid the doctor with vegetables from the garden). Bessie administered steam inhalers night and day to help him breath. It was touch and go whether he would survive but he gradually pulled through and was able to live to carry out his mothers wish that he should find the Cork family and thank them. Jack died in 2011.

Walter was to go on and have a large family of fourteen, twelve of whom survived, six girls and six boys. After Walter's death his family arranged a Christmas party every year. Next year, 2022 will be the 50th anniversary of that Christmas party. There are usually ninety to one hundred and twenty attending.

On Walters first day home from France and the war, his daughter Molly, who had been conceived whilst he was home some eighteen months earlier convalescing, walked for her very first time to meet him.

That little girl was my mum,
Walter was my grandfather

Molly Jean Knell

1918 - 1994

CHINDIT

ALAN LINDSAY GOODHEW

LANCE CORPORAL
6018303

ESSEX REGIMENT

"I was born in May 1919 in Narrogin, Australia, which is a small country town 140 miles south east of Perth. My parents and grandparents were farming 1000 acres of corn, agriculture and sheep. I had my own pony that I rode about the farm. Later, when I started school I had to ride a horse ten miles to get there, I then placed him in a paddock till I finished for the day, then ride him home. When my grandfather died the farm was sold and my parents moved to Borden, Sittingbourne in Kent, England".

Alan on the right with his mother and older brother

Alan went to Borden school, left aged 15 and did an apprenticeship as a trainee hairdresser with Bill Mantral in Sittingbourne. On finishing his apprenticeship he moved to Southend Essex to work at 'Masonoopers' as the manager of one of their shops.

"I was asked to go back and work the farm in Australia and actually made arrangements to go back. But then the war broke out in 1939. The government had brought in conscription then and you had to report to the Labour Exchange, so that's where I reported. They asked for my birth certificate and I told them I didn't have one. They said "Of course you have one". I said "Well I might have but I don't know where it is". When they said that I would have to get one I told them I couldn't because I was born in Australia. They then said "If you were born in Australia you don't come under the conscription here, Australia doesn't have conscription". They told me I could join as a volunteer, so that's what I did.

"Later I had a letter telling me to report to Portsmouth for the Royal Navy. I thought to myself I don't fancy the Navy, so I wrote back saying I had no wish to join the Navy and that I wanted to go to Borley Barracks in Essex where all my friends were joining up". I subsequently received a letter saying in that case I didn't have to join the Navy and I should report to Borley Barracks. I joined Borley on the same day as my friends. They asked if anyone had knowledge of Morse Code, I told them I did, I had learned it in the Boy Scouts as a boy. They tested me and were impressed and told me I would be in the Signals".

"After three months training, I was promoted to Lance Corporal. I was put in charge of a platoon and we had to guard places like Canvey Island Oil Refinery and a RAF station in Essex. I thought I'm fed up with this, so when they put a notice on the notice board asking if anyone wanted to join the Essex regiment in the Middle East, I and several friends volunteered, we were to replace the casualties fighting the Germans. Because of the threat of the U-Boats we flew from Scotland to America then on to Free Town in Africa. From there to Cape Town and then on to Egypt. In Egypt we were told we would be joining the Essex's in Ethiopia. We went down the river Nile to a crossing where we caught a train down to Khartoum".

First Battle Ethiopia.
"I met up with the regiment who were fighting the Italians. They were holding a fort and our colonel made the decision to make a direct approach on it. We had no tanks or heavy artillery but we did have mortars, however the colonel didn't use them at our disgust and we all thought he must be a nut case and that we will never break the walls of the fort. We suffered very heavy casualties and were withdrawn. The colonel was dismissed and was pensioned off!"

Lance corporal Goodhew abroad on the right

"After that we went up to the RAF base in Habbiniya in Iraq, which was about 55 miles west of Baghdad. We were guarding the base because it was being bombed by the Germans and they thought it was to be attacked. We were there for a few months and it was very hot. We were finally relieved by the Gurkha's because we told we were going into Syria. At that time it was occupied by the French Foreign legion under German control. We were told that if we captured any of them we were to treat them as POWs but they would be sent back to France. We went in and over ran the first fort, we put a few mortar bombs into it and up came the white flag. We then went north and did the same to the next one, they also surrendered.

Seige of Tobruk
The Australians were fighting the Germans in North Africa, when they fell back to Tobruk and dug in to defend it against the Italians and Germans operating under Lt. Gen. Erwin Rommel. We joined the Australians in defending Tobruk. German propaganda called us Rats, and that is where the name 'Desert Rats' comes from. We held Tobruk for 241 days under constant shelling and bombing until we had to break out. Our supplies had to come in at night on the river. We were told that a South African Division was going to push up and we were to take a ridge called 'El Duda' and hold it for three days until they linked up with the 8th Army. But Rommel had different ideas and put a tank division round the back of us. Shelled and bombed we were held up for seventeen days not three and we lost 40% of our unit. The Black Watch were worse off than us having lost 50% of their men taking the ridge. I was shot in the hip, the medics patched me up and I carried on. On another occasion I was talking to my second in command, Lt. Baker when a mortar bomb dropped between us. I was sitting down and he was standing up, the angle it came in at meant that he caught more of the blast than me. We were both blown into the air, he went higher than me. I landed in the hole and my mates pulled me out asking if I was alright, Lt. Baker was dead. The shock of the blast gave me jaundice.

Jaundice
Of course because we were cut off I couldn't get any treatment. For nearly two weeks I couldn't eat anything and could only drink water and bring up green bile and all under constant shelling and bombing. Over in the valley we could see some tents, we watched them through binoculars for several days and could see no movement. So we decided to go down and

have a look. After a cautious approach we found it deserted, it turned out to be a German supply depot. I took a pair of goggles to keep the sand out my eyes and a large tin of something but didn't know what it was. When we got back with the other lads we got the tin open and found it to be turkey meat, so they all had some with their biscuits, I couldn't eat anything, not even a bight. In the third week we began to break through and I was told to make my way over to the ridge where a supply lorry should give me a lift into Tobruk. I was given a letter to be able to board a ship but when I boarded they said there was no spare accommodation. I spent the whole time on the upper deck. Having got to a field hospital in Egypt I was told to dump my clothes, have a shower and don some pyjamas. The Doctor, having been told I had been like this for three weeks, told me mush longer and we would be burying you. Whilst in hospital I was joined by a mate of mine. We were sitting up in bed one day when a famous singer visited, it was Vera Lynn. She stopped and spoke to my mate. She said "Hello Sid, what are you doing in here"? Sid then introduced her to me. Afterwards I asked Sid how he knew her and he said that he went to school with her.

I was feeling better and wanted to get out. I spoke to one of the drivers of a supply lorry and asked him where the 70th Division and the 23rd Brigade was he told me they were just up the road and the Essex's were a bit further on. It is rumoured that they are going to Singapore. I thought, they are not going without me! I asked him for a lift, he said he's not allowed to but he would leave the back door open on the van, sit on the floor but lock the door. The Sergeant wanted to see my discharge papers, I told him I didn't have them. He knew Id discharged myself and told me that as he knew me he would put me on the strength and 'lose my papers'. A few days later we boarded a ship for Singapore, however a few days out at sea the Tannoy announced that we will not be going to Singapore as it had fallen to the Japanese last night (15th

February 1942) we would be heading for Bombay.

India and Burma, the Battle at Kohima
We landed in Bombay and were told we were going to Poona, Southern India to be kitted out, we would then be going up North to the Burmese border. The Japanese had advanced up to Kohima which is the first town in India next the Burmese border. The Japanese had taken a hill over looking the town and they wanted us to take that hill. The Japanese had dug deep into the hill and covered the holes with bushes so it was difficult to see them.

One of the Kent Regiments, I think it might have been the Buffs, had the job of taking the hill and we were to stop any Jap reinforcements coming in. The Kent regiment attacked and suffered heavy losses and had to withdraw. They were told they had to take the hill and attacked it again but suffered more losses and were pulled out.

Someone had a brainwave idea and went down to the town and found a bulldozer. He then got a piece of metal sheet and had it welded along the front of it. He drove this up the hill and dropped the scoop at the front and by driving back and forth buried the Japs alive in their fox holes!

Chindits
After that we were sent for jungle warfare training and formed as Chindits, a special long penetration group designed to attack the Japs deep behind their lines.

I was living in Burma as a wireless operator, a group of us were in the Jungle hiding up in some bamboo when a villager told us that in the valley up the road there a load of Japs. Our commander told us we were going to go up there and surprise them. So we went up there with some of the lads and some Bren gunners. We found them and opened fire, we must have killed a lot of them but then they came back firing like mad and we were told to withdraw. Having got back on the road we did

a head count and found we were one man short.
The Commander said "its too risky to go back for one man".

Alan third from the left. The Burmese jungle behind them.

So I said "Well I'm not going back without him". The commander asked if I knew him and I told him I didn't know who he was but that he was out there somewhere and I'm taking this unit back. In the end they all went off and I went off into the jungle to find him.

I was crawling about in the bushes saying "Is there anyone there....Is there anyone there"?

Then a reply came "Yes it's me I'm shot in the thigh"

I crawled over to him and told him to get on my back and I'd crawl up the hill. While doing this the Japs were firing randomly through the bushes. We made it over the hill and onto the track and made our way back. When I got over there my mate Sid was waiting for me. He said he had been waiting for me. He gave me a hand to carry this lad back. When we got back to the bamboo place we were staying at we handed him over to a medic. I never did know the name of that lad. I was mentioned in despatches for this.

On another occasion at the bamboo place, the Japs knew we were there, they would shout out to us in English "Come out

Tommy we won't hurt you"!

We ignored them until one day they had taken a prisoner, they were sticking their bayonets into him and getting him to shout to us. He was screaming "Help, Help" and they carried on stabbing him.

The Major who was in charge at the time said "I'm going to call for a plane to bomb the area, I'd rather he was killed than he put up with this.

A plane came in and bombed the area and all went quiet. We went looking for him and shouting "Are you alive"? And eventually he shouted back "Yes". Some of the Japs had been killed and the rest scarpered leaving this lad alone. He had fourteen stab wounds but was still alive.

A light plane was called for to transport him out. We placed him behind the pilot but because of the short runway in the jungle clearing he was going to find it difficult to take off loaded. So what we did, we all held on to the wings and tail plane whilst the pilot revved the engine hard, when the pilot waved we all let go and off he roared just clearing the trees. We later heard that he had survived.

We had several skirmishes against the Japs in Burma. We approached a village one day but were uncertain as to whether there were any Japs there. Our officer wasn't going to stick his neck out and suggested we wait to see if there's any movement. I suggested to my mate Sid that we each take a flank, keep in the jungle and meet up the other side. I was waiting for Sid to join me when a Burmese villager runs towards me holding up three fingers and saying, "Japanese, Japanese". I waited and then saw three Japs coming towards me, I jumped up with my Sten gun, went to fire and it went 'Click', I couldn't unjam it and the Japs were taking there guns off their shoulder slings to shoot at me... then I heard a quick burst of gunfire, one Jap fell dead and the other two ran off wounded into the jungle. Lucky for me it was Sid, He said "Seems I arrived just in time"!

We took the ID tag off this Jap for intelligence, it stated they were men from His Majesty's Imperial Guards, a crack regiment.

In the man's pocket was a photo of his wife and a boy about ten years old both in traditional costume, we put it back in his pocket. Sid said, "The difference between us and them is that his family will be highly rewarded for his death, but if we die our families get nothing"

Wireless operations

They wanted wireless operators to go behind the lines and live with the Burmese, so Sid and I volunteered and spent some months in a village several hundred miles behind the lines. We had a Lieutenant of the Burmese army with us as an interpreter, he dressed as, and lived as the Burmese. The bamboo huts, Bashers, we lived in were three feet off the ground to keep them out of the monsoon rains. The villagers built us a secret room in the back of one of the huts where Sid and I could operate the radio. The Burmese officer would travel to different villages to gather intelligence, he would then bring it to us. He would tell us how many Japs there were and where they were headed. We had a map and would transmit this back to India in Morse code.

The Americans would occasionally drop K rations to us, you got three small bars, one bar of 3000 calories per meal, our stomachs were shrinking all the time. We ate mainly just rice but there wasn't much of that, the Japs were stealing the villages rice so they didn't have much.

The Japs would come through the village sometimes saying to the villages in broken English, "Englasie, Englasie". The villagers were good, they would say, "No, no, no English in this village". The villagers did not give you away because in one village where they admitted there were English, the villagers were shot as well for harbouring them.

Eventually we were met by an army group and we trekked out

of there. I was in a sorry state walking out of there, I made two crutches to help me walk. When we got back to India I was told to shave of my long beard, cut off my hair and have a shower. Then I jumped on the scales, I weighed just 4st 4lbs! I was given a railway warrant and told to make my way back to Bombay. Because I had now been overseas for five and a half years and everybody over five were being sent home.

Thirty of our group had gone into the jungle...just ten came out alive.

1944

We were on the boat leaving and we said to each other, "When we get back we should get a nice job in the depot". Did we heck! We were disgusted, after a few weeks we were sent off to Germany.

Malaria

I didn't go straight away because I went down with Malaria. I was put in the Reading Military hospital. There I got friendly with one of the nurses and took her out for afternoon tea on her day off. I recovered and was sent back to my unit so back to the hospital I went. There I saw Liz, the nurse again, She said "I knew you wouldn't be able to keep away". Over time I got better and was sent to Germany. Liz asked if we could keep in touch and I told her yes.

Germany

In Germany I had another spell of Malaria and was declared unfit for for front line service. So I was sent to a unit outside Hanover. This used to be a Spa for the rich and famous, including King George 5th, but was taken over by the military as a prison for high profile Nazis. I was on the staff there. In the cells we had prisoners like Irma Grese, nicknamed 'The beautiful beast'. Another was Joseph Kramer, formerly commandant of Auschwitz and Belson concentration camps, he was known as the 'Beast of Belson'. We used to put two in each cell, which was bugged. There German Jewish women who had joined the British in the ATS who listened in and recorded the conversations in short hand. This was to gather evidence for the forthcoming trials.

The commanding officer then had me and another cutting peoples hair. On my Sundays off I was able to go to the former German Army officers stables and take a beautiful horse for a ride in the Black Forest.

Demobbed

When I finally got my demob an officer lined us up and he gave out our medals, but I told the officer I didn't want mine, they didn't have my name on them and they could be anyone's. I and several others threw them on the ground. However some time later the M.o.D, posted them to me, but still without my name on them.

He had survived, Luck Fate, or was it writ?

Chindits badge Alan wore on his blazer

Alan and his nurse Liz married and finally settled in Bannister Hall, Borden, Sittingbourne in Kent. Alan went into a nursery business with his father. They went on to have five children, four girls and one boy.

Alan with 'nurse' and wife Liz..

Fond memories of granddad....Stuart.

ILLUSTRATIONS INDEX

Addison, Den..........................25
Army lorry............................73
Bahnpong station..................103
Bombed house Ilkiston..........33
Boxing, POW camp..............91
Buffs badge..........................89
Buffs non comm, officers.......117
Bullen HMS..........................45
Call up papers......................36
Cavalier HMS........................5
Cemetery Thai......................113
Chalmondley Castle.............49
Chalmondley hospital ward...51
Chindits badge......................133
Cork Walter Frederick............116
Danzig, map..........................90
Davis, Dave..........................53
Delight, HMS..........................60
DEMs gunners badge............26
Destroyer Memorial...............5
Discharge papers..................43
Dixon post card......................119
Drawings, of Charlies Op.......66,67,68,69
Evacuating troops..................38
Fisher, Alan and mother.........88
Germans fleeing, Danzig.......95
Goodhew Alan.....................122, 123,125, 129
Graves, Ballagen...................24
Guest William.........................98
Guest W. diary........................99
Guest William news cutting....113
Hardy HMS (I)........................7
Hardy HMS, Suicide squad...21
Hardy HMS wreck.................16
Hardy HMS(II)......................79
Holness, Doreen...................58
Knell, Charlie.........................63,76
Knell Charlie's photo fames...77
Knell, Hector..........................35
Knell Molly.............................122

Lentaigne, Mollie.................66
Liz, nurse
Map of Southwick Tunnels....74
Map South Atlantic...............29
Map Tunis..............................42
Marienburg castle.................96
Medals, Hectors....................43
Medway HMS.......................54
Molly Knell............................122
Mounsey HMS.......................85
Narvik, destruction at............15
Narvik harbour......................24
Open boat..............................28
POW photographs................91,92,93
Presentation to Les...............22
Royal Corps Signals, badge..64
Royal West Kent, badge........37
Ship torpedoed......................27
Smale, Les.............................6
Stage Play, POW camp........91
Starving POW.......................105
Tank Traps............................64
Tankard, Mapin & Webb.......76
Tegleberg SS.......................110
Tegleberg lounge.................110
Telegraph pole.....................70
Thunderbolt HM Sub............55
Torpedoed merchant ship.....27
Troops in lorry......................38
Tunnel entrance steps.........75
Wild Swan HMS.................40

INDEX

Abbey Street, Faversham...63
Addison, Denis... 25
Africa...56
Akureyi... 81
Albert...39
Alexander, Egypt...55
Algiers...41
Amiens...117
Arras...117
Ascot...98
Asprey...104
Auschwitz...132
Australia...122
Baghdad...125
Bahnpong...103
Baker, Lt...126
Bakewell...100
Ballangen...18, 19
Bango...105
Bannister Hall...133
Bapaume...117
Barnsley...112
Battleaxe – Operation...41
Bay of Biscay...78
Beaney, Bessie...115
BEF...87
Belson...132
Bilsington...115
Black Forest...133
Blandford barracks...35
Bobbing...116
Bombay...100,128,132
Borley, Barracks...124
Borden...122
Boulogne...39
Brazil...31
Buffs...115,128
Bullen HMS...45,50,51
Burma...99,128

Cambell Cpt....81
Canvey Island...124
Cape San Vito Bay...55
Cape town...124
Cape Wrath...50,51,80
Carnoy...117
Catterick, barracks...64,100
Cavalier HMS...5,78
Chalmondley Castle...49
Changi...102,109
Charybdis HMS...79
Chatham – barracks...47,48
Chatham Historic Dockyard..52
Cherbourg...85
Cherisy...118
Chindits...128
Christianson, Mrs...18
Cholera Hill...106
Chumleigh Castle...49
Churchill W...23,74
Clark Lt...12
Cleethorpes...84
Conyer...64
Corinthia SS...55
Clarke Nobby...102
Cork Molly...63
Cork Eliz, George...115
Cork Walter...115,116
Crewe...47
Cullen Frances...116
Danzig...93,94,89
D-Day...72
Davis, Cyril...53
Deal...77
Delight HMS...58
Dickenson, Ken...79
Dido HMS...55
Dixon McDonald...120
Djebel Aliod...42

Dolphin HMS...54
Dorset...72
Doullens..38,39,43,87,88,96
Dover...40,70
Dunkirk...39,87,99
Dunluce Castle HMS...79
East Grinstead...65
East Kent Reg.(Buffs)...37
Edinburgh Duke of...4
Egypt...127
Eisenhower...74
El Duda...126
Empress of Japan MV...100
Ethiopia...124
Faulkner HMS...61
Faversham...63
Fisher, Alan...43,88
Flotta...80
Fort Southwick...73
Fort Widley...73
France...99
Franconia SS...20
Freetown...124
Frevent..38
Gawber...100
Gdansk...89
Germany...132
Gloworm HMS...8
Gneisenau BM...9
Goodall HMS...52
Goodhew Alan...122,123,125
Greenstreet...115
Grese, Irma...132
Guinea Pig Club...69
Habbiniya...125
Hall Ben...116
Hall, Jim...45
Hall 'Nobby'...84
Hardy HMS...6,9,15,21,24
Harwood, Admrl...55
Havock HMS...9
Hazebrouke...117
Heppel, Lt....19

Hero HMS...20
Hesperus HMS...52
HG84 - convoy...44
Hipper...8
Holland John...116
Holness, Doreen,Nurse...61
Hostile HMS...11
Hotspur HMS...7
Hovenden...8
HRH Duke of Edinburgh...24
Hunter HMS...7,9
Iceland...81,82
Ilkeston...25
Impulsive HMS...80,84
Indeled...23
India...128
Invicta Park – barracks...35
Iraq...125
Isle of Man...37
Isle of Lewis...50
Isle of Sheppey...63,78
Isle of Skye...45
Ivanhoe HMS...19
Jarmans, boatyard...64
JW56A – convoy...80
JW56B – convoy...81
Kadish Ruth...101
Kampong...104
Kings College Hospital...61
Kingsferry Bridge...77
Knell Hector...35,43,89,96
Knell Jesse...35
Knell, Charlie...63
Knell David...41
Knell Madeline...43
Knell Molly...121
Knell Roger...96
Kohima...128
Kola Inlet...81,83,86
Kramer...132
Kwai river...99,106
Lady of Man MV...37
Lafoten...10

138

Lawrence, G...61
Le Havre...37
Lee 'Colonal'...84
Lentaigne, Mollie...65
Leysdown...64
Lincolnshire...72
Liverpool...55
Lock Ewe...80
lofoton Isles...10
Louviers...37
Lynn, Vera...127
Malaya...99
Malbork, Poland...88,89
Mantral, Bill...123
Marharrata HMS...80
Marienburg, East Prussia..89
Masonoopers...123
Mateur...42
McCracken Mr RN...17
McIndoe, Archibald...65
Medway HMS...54,55,56
Milne HMS...81
Montauban...117
Montigny...120
Morgan, 'Rattler'...60
Mounsey HMS...85
Murmansk...82,87
Mountbatten Admrl...110
Narrogin...122
Narvik...6,10,11,18,20,21,22
Natal...31
Neame Cpt...117
Newfoundland...85
Newmann, Heinz, Cdr...55
Nogat river...92
Onslow HMS...85
Operation Hannibal...95
Operation Torch...41
Operation Wilfred...8,23
Orchard View...41
Ould, Vic...52
Outram gaol...111
Outer Hebrides...80

Pakenham HMS...56
Panang...101
Paris – Liner...37
Parish, Lt. Cdr...52
Peitrermaritzberg...57
Pembroke HMS...53
Pernambuco...32
Perry, a friend...104
Perth...122
Pilangie, village...31
Pimperne...35
Polyarnoe...84,86
Pont de Larche...37
Poona...128
Port Said...55
Portland Bill...58,60
Portsmouth...73,74,124
Prai...103
Primula HMS...53
Queenborough...64
Queen Victoria Hospital...65
Quested Jesse...35
Raffles Square...110
Reading,Hospital...132
Red Cross...97
Renown HMS...8,9
Robson, Cpt....82
Rommel, Gen...55,126
Rouen...37
Rouple, Brigadier...38,39
Rouquenet Wood...117
Royal Albert Docks...54
Royal Corps Signals...64
Royal Engineers...73
Royal West Kents...87,35,38
Safi...41
Sardinia...62
Scapa...9,81
Scharnhorst BM...9
Selerang...103
Shaw Peter...86
Sheerness...64
Sheffield...102

Shepherd writer RN...61
Shetlands...6,7
Siam...99
Singapore...70,127
Sittingbourne...54,57
Skegness...53
Smale, Les...6,21
Smith, Ken...84
Southend...123
Spanish fishermen...44
Spells, Fred...96
Stalag XXB...88
Stammelager...89
Stanning Lt...14,15
Stoke Canon...21
Stord, Norwegian Dest....79,84
Stornaway...80
Strafe, punishment...92
Stuart...134
Sullam Voe...7
Sungie Patani...101
Sunkrai...105
Sunningdale...98
Sweden...23
Syria...125
Taunton...71
Teynham...63,76
Tegleberg...85,111
Thetis HM Sub...55
Thunderbolt HM Sub...54
Tilbury Docks...41
Tobruk...126
Tonge Mill...35
Torch – Operation...41
Trondheim...51
Tunis...41
Tyne HMS...80
U372...55
U-775...51
Vaenga...84,86
Venus HMS...80,83
West Street Faversham...63
Wiggs Shop...76

Virago HMS...82
Warburton-Lee Cpt...22
Warspite HMS...19
Whitehall HMS...85
Wicks, Mr...41
Wicks bakery...35
Wilcockson Nigel, letter...118,120
Wild Swan HMS...43,40
Wilfred, Operation...8
Wilhelm Gustoff SS...96
Willenberg...89
Yasumi...106
York Minster...83
Ypre...117

Author

Barry Knell

Barry was the next to eldest of eleven children. Born to Molly and Charlie in 1939 in Teynham, he still remembers quite clearly some of the dog fights high in the sky, the low flying doodlebugs, the bombing, air raids, and the eery sirens of WWII. He joined the Royal Navy in 1957, to avoid being called up for National Service, and having to serve as a 'Brown Job', (army). Having enjoyed travelling all over the world and having got married in 1965, he left the navy in 1966. He has two daughters and four grand children. He spent two years trying a variety of jobs, and then joined the Kent County Constabulary in 1969. Having served a full on, but very interesting twenty four years he retired in 1992.

Other books by this author,

'THE FASTEST SHIP IN THE FLEET', THE STORY OF HMS CAVALIER AND HER MEN.
Published and produced by the Chatham Historic Dockyard Trust. ISBN 978-0-9534260-1-0
'WIPED, BUT NOT CLEAN' MY POLCING IN KENT.
Published by, Compass Publishing.
Printed by New Perspective, Digital Print. ISBN 978-1-913713-56-0